The

A V ᴀʟ Agent

The Life of Sir George Macartney

18 January 1867-19 May 1945

James McCarthy

The subject of this biography, Sir George Macartney, was of mixed Scottish-Chinese parentage. Based in remote Kashgar on the famous Silk Road, he was caught up in the great 19th and early 20th century power-struggle among Britain, China and Russia over control of Central Asia in what came to be known as 'The Great Game'. Here he met the scheming Russian Consul Nicolai Petrovsky who was to prove a cunning adversary in the political contest for control in this turbulent region. Much of the book is concerned with Petrovsky's devious machinations to outflank the British agent. Macartney's wife, Catherine, has provided intimate descriptions of their domestic life and some of the hazardous journeys they made with their family when travelling to and from the United Kingdom on leave. Her very few visitors were unstinting in their praise for her courage and adaptability, not least when seriously threatened by revolutionaries. They also recognised that only George Macartney, with his renowned tact and diplomacy, allied to steely determination, could have maintained the British position with so little external support. His dangerous encounter leading a mission to the Bolshevik revolutionaries in Tashkent made for a dramatic finale to his extraordinary career in a restive region now causing concern to the Chinese government.

The Author, James McCarthy was born in Dundee, Scotland in 1936, graduated from Aberdeen University in 1959 and now lives in Edinburgh. He saw military service with the Royal Marines, Black Watch and King's African Rifles during the Mau Mau campaign in Kenya. Subsequently he became the first European post-graduate student at Makerere College, Kampala and carried out forest exploration in Uganda and Tanzania, latterly introducing the first course in forest ecology for African forest rangers. He has been the holder of a Leverhulme Scholarship, a Churchill Fellowship and a Nuffield-Leverhulme Fellowship. He has travelled widely in Europe, North America, Africa and Australia. He retired as Deputy Director (Scotland) from the Nature Conservancy Council in 1991 and became a Board Member of the new organisation, Scottish Natural Heritage. His consultancy work has included advising the Icelandic Government on interpretation for visitors to their first National Park and US National Park Service on coastal conservation. He has published books on the natural heritage and land use of Scotland and, latterly, biographies of 18th and 19th Century Scottish explorers and travellers, in whom he has a special interest. He is currently chairman of the Scottish Centre for Geopoetics. He is married, with three grown-up children.

The Diplomat of Kashgar
A Very Special Agent

The Life of Sir George Macartney
18 January 1867-19 May 1945

James McCarthy

Proverse Hong Kong

The Diplomat of Kashgar: A Very Special Agent:
The Life of Sir George Macartney
18 January 1867-19 May 1945
by James McCarthy.
2nd pbk edition published in Hong Kong by Proverse Hong Kong,
August 2015. Copyright © Proverse Hong Kong, August 2015.
ISBN: 978-988-8228-14-0
Printed by CreateSpace.

1st published in pbk in Hong Kong by Proverse Hong Kong, November
2014.
Copyright © Proverse Hong Kong, 20 November 2014.
ISBN: 978-988-8227-62-4
Distribution (Hong Kong and worldwide):
The Chinese University Press of Hong Kong, The Chinese University
of Hong Kong, Shatin, New Territories, Hong Kong SAR.
E-mail: cup-bus@cuhk.edu.hk; Web: www.chineseupress.com
Tel: [INT+852] 3943-9800; Fax: [INT+852] 2603-7355
Distribution (United Kingdom):
Christine Penney, Stratford-upon-Avon, Warwickshire CV37 6DN,
England. Email: <chrisp@proversepublishing.com>
Distribution and other enquiries to:
Proverse Hong Kong, P.O. Box 259, Tung Chung Post Office, Tung
Chung, Lantau Island, NT, Hong Kong SAR, China.
E-mail: proverse@netvigator.com; Web: www.proversepublishing.com

The right of James McCarthy to be identified as the author of this work
has been asserted by him
in accordance with the Copyright, Designs and Patents Act 1988.

Cover design by Artist Hong Kong Company
and Proverse Hong Kong. Page design by Proverse Hong Kong.

British Library Cataloguing in Publication Data.
A catalogue record for this book is available from the British Library.

ACKNOWLEDGEMENTS

I am indebted to Dumfries & Galloway Library for historic material relating to the Macartneys of Galloway and to Bright 3D Design for the redrawing of maps. I owe special thanks to Kwan Sau Ming for her research in untangling the nomenclature of Chinese officials in the period. Finally, I am grateful to Graham Leicester for contributing a most appropriate foreword to this work.

PERMISSIONS

The following are published with the permission of the Library and Information Centre of the Hungarian Academy of Sciences (LHAS):
Macartney with his wife and three children (Cat. Stein LHAS 19/29 Chinibagh group, Les Vaux, Sept 19, 1920 [G.])
Mrs (later Lady) Macartney sitting in the Chini Bagh garden, Kashgar, c.1901, shortly after her arrival there. (Cat.Stein. LHAS 44/1 (9).)
Macartney Family (Cat.Stein LHAS 44/1 (7).) George and Catherine Macartney and staff on the verandah of Chini Bagh, Kashgar, c.1901. George Macartney wears a mourning arm-band, presumably after the death of Queen Victoria.
George (later, Sir George) Macartney at Chini Bagh, Kashgar (Cat.Stein. LHAS 44/1 (8).) Portrait of George Macartney, British Consul at Kashgar, 1900s.
Aurel Stein (Cat.Stein LHAS 29(28).)

The following are published with permission; Copyright © The British Library Board (BLB), All Rights Reserved:
Macartney with Colonel Francis Younghusband, Henry Lennard and Richard Beech (The British Library Board: Oriental and India Collection. BL source: Mss Eur F197/674(1), P14.)
Colonel Francis Younghusband. (The British Library Board: Eileen Younghusband Collection. BL source: Mss Eur F197/646 (13), P17.)

IN THE PUBLIC DOMAIN:
View of Kashgar, 1878. Taken from Robert Shaw, Visits to High Tartary...., 1871. Licensed under the terms of the GNU Free Documentation License.
Kashgar Road Scene showing different modes of transport on the Silk Road. Sketch by T.E. Gordon, 1870. (Wikimedia)

The maps are based on maps in C.P. Skrine, *Macartney at Kashgar,* Methuen, 1973, redrawn by Ewan McCarthy, Bright 3D Design.

For Jill, for her encouragement and patience

'There is no British Consul in Kashgar, but Mr. George Macartney, Special Agent to the Resident in Kashmir for Chinese Affairs, is stationed there. If it were of any urgency to communicate with him, it is possible to get a telegram through in three or four days, via Pekin, but in this case we have to telegraph to Her Majesty's Minister in Pekin, who sends the wire over the Chinese wire. This is very seldom done and is not always safe. Ordinarily we should send instructions to Mr. Macartney through the Resident in Kashmir who would wire it to Gilgit, whence the message would go on to Kashgar by dak runners, arriving in about a fortnight.'[1]

**Sir George Macartney in the garden of Chini Bagh,
his official residence in Kashgar.**

FOREWORD

"The Diplomat of Kashgar". There is something magical in the phrase, bound to stir the imagination, particularly if you are British and have any sense of history. It speaks of remote and dangerous places. It brings to mind tales of adventure and intrigue in the 'Great Game' for strategic supremacy in Central Asia between the British and Russian empires at the turn of the twentieth century. It conjures images of distant lands and forgotten empires along the ancient Silk Road from China to India and the West. It is a setting that has provided the backdrop for endless stories of adventure and 'derring do' over the centuries, featuring soldiers, secret agents, traders, travellers and all kinds of extraordinary individual adventurers. On this most remarkable of stages, crowded with eye-catching performers, what role might the humble diplomat play?

It is a virtue of James McCarthy's book that it satisfies all of these different interests and curiosities. His story of Sir George Macartney "representing British interests, almost unsupported and in the face of determined opposition for twenty-eight years in one of the most inaccessible posts in the service of the British Government" (as one of Macartney's successors, Sir Clarmont Percival Skrine, put it) contains all the elements you would expect. It is a tale of intrigue and suspense, hardship and homesickness, geopolitics and high policy.

It is also the story of another age. Inevitably there is a tinge of nostalgia as Macartney finally leaves Kashgar in affectionate triumph at the end of a posting that had begun in 1890 "eulogised alike by officials, merchants and ordinary people". He travelled home through a war-torn Europe changed utterly in 1918 which must have seemed very strange to a man who had left its shores at the age of twenty (and who had spent the first ten years of his life in

China). Macartney retired to Jersey, away from the hurly burly. Yet there was no escaping the rush of modernity: the island was occupied by Germany in the second world war and Macartney died a few days after liberation in 1945.

At the same time this is a story that still has relevance today. The 'Great Game' in Central Asia goes on. The region of Xinjiang, where Kashgar is the second city, sits at the heart of one of the least stable parts of the globe, bordering Russia, the Central Asian republics, Kashmir, Afghanistan, Pakistan. It has been a disputed territory for centuries, finally incorporated into China only in the 18th century. Its name means "new border", a reference to its strategic importance as a buffer zone in China's remote North West – originally against Russia seeking to play a greater Eurasian role, now equally against the threat of Islamic insurgency spreading across the border to the minority Uighur population, chafing against Beijing rule and allegedly responsible for recent acts of separatist violence.

Equally the region is reassuming strategic importance as a route of connection – an increasingly important overland trading route to Europe and strategically important as an alternative to China's eastern seaboard for supply and support – not to mention the valuable deposits of coal and other rare minerals now becoming both essential and accessible. If, as many believe, this is to be China's century, then Macartney's old stomping ground will have an important part to play.

This book, and the history it helps bring to mind, is thus a useful source of knowledge and insight into a region we can expect to hear about a lot more. But it is also, and for my part more importantly, a reminder of what a difference the traditional skills of diplomacy can make in a fraught situation in the person of a skilled practitioner.

It is tempting to see in Macartney's story the familiar caricature of the 'stiff upper lip' and inscrutable British behaviour of the 'ripping yarns' variety. That is certainly here, and authentic. With China rocked by revolution in

1912, for example, the British community in Kashgar feared for their lives. As Macartney's wife Catherine recalls: "our servants armed themselves with any kind of weapon they could find... knives, sticks, old swords etc... and even our governess Miss Cresswell took the big carving knife and steel to bed with her... Having made all preparations possible we lay down fully dressed while Donald and Mr Hunter took it in turns to do sentry duty round the house and garden". The night passed quietly, the threat of rebellion faded and Macartney, his brother and his eight-year old son took to riding daily through the city together simply to demonstrate their trust that no harm would come to them.

We can read the narrative likewise as confirming our impression of turn of the century British diplomacy as complacently caught between two worlds, wedded to a policy of "masterly inactivity" as the tectonic plates of international politics began to shift. Macartney is typical of the beleaguered official far from home. His consulate was said to fly the only Union Jack between India and the North Pole and his wife met only three of her fellow countrywomen in Kashgar during her fourteen years there and none in her first decade. As Russia begins to assert its position and China shows signs of dramatic shifts at the end of the Manchu era, Macartney is constantly urging his superiors to pay more attention to the area, always asking for instructions that never come, looking for financial and other support (Macartney quotes Sir Ernest Satow's *Guide to Diplomatic Practice* to the effect that a private income is very desirable and "the higher the grade, the more of it the better"), and struggling to maintain authority locally without the necessary recognition and status from his capital (he was officially recognised as His Britannic Majesty's Consul only in 1908).

Yet at the same time, those who meet him, from Colonel Younghusband, who first took him to Kashgar as an interpreter for the various visiting archaeologists led by Sir Aurel Stein, entranced by his collections and his hospitality to later intrepid travellers, special agents and military men, all comment on his exceptional personal qualities and achievements. One such traveller, Miss E.G. Kemp, was asked by fifteen hundred British Indians to tell the Foreign Secretary, Sir Edward Grey that, "if it had not been for Sir G. Macartney, Russia would long ago have swallowed up the whole country".

It was the exquisite subtlety of his handling of personal relationships, particularly with the Chinese, and his wider awareness of the international context beyond the immediate issue, that were so impressive. Half-Chinese himself, Macartney evidently understood from his time in a British public school (Dulwich College, my own alma mater) and in the Diplomatic Service what it is to feel marginalised and not accepted. (Younghusband notes that "Macartney is a good enough fellow in his way but he is not English.") Add to this natural empathy his instinctive appreciation of the importance of face, of symbolic action and of relationship in Chinese culture, plus courage in abundance, a love of good conversation and a sharp inquiring mind, and you have pretty much the ideal diplomat for that time and those surroundings. Indeed for any time, and any surroundings. There is much we could learn today from what one colleague at the time called "his dispassionate methods of reasoning, his quiet careful habits of observation, and his experienced tact in dealing with Chinese officials".

Today the area of Xinjiang is covered from the British Embassy in Beijing. It is a plane ride away. Doubtless we stay 'in touch' by monitoring the local press, reading economic reports (Kashgar is now designated a Special Economic Zone of the People's Republic of China), gleaning data from other sources, friends and allies. Macartney's story is a tribute to an older tradition of diplomacy, a world of human relationship, character and sound, universal values. Macartney 'served British interests' by keeping the peace in the region between Russia and China. His greatest achievement was to release thousands of local British Indians from slavery. He was able to do this not because he was delivering a particularly enlightened policy, but because he personally won the respect and admiration locally of all who came to know him. In this he was faithfully supported throughout by his equally adventurous wife, who set off for Central Asia with him in 1898 with (in her own words) "no qualifications for a pioneer's life beyond being able to make a cake".

Macartney's character shines through this book. James McCarthy has performed a great service by bringing to light the remarkable achievements of this quiet, humble and highly effective exemplar of a style of diplomacy we neglect at our peril.

Graham Leicester
HM Diplomatic Service, 1984 - 1995

CONTENTS

TABLE OF ILLUSTRATIONS

AUTHOR'S INTRODUCTION

George Macartney was, in Jeanette Mirsky's words, 'by any measure a most unusual man ...child of a most improbable marriage, a Scottish father and an upper class Chinese mother.'[2] The name Macartney is but one of several variants of McCarthy, the original thought to be McCarthy More [sic] (or the 'Great McCarthy') from Munster in Ireland, whose youngest son Donald McCarthy welcomed Edward Bruce, brother of the more famous Robert de Bruce, after the Scottish victory at Bannockburn. But after Edward's defeat and death at Dundalk, the Scots and many of their Irish supporters retreated to Scotland, initially to Argyll and subsequently to Galloway in southwest Scotland, establishing a stronghold around Loch Urr in the present parish of Kirkpatrick-Durham.

In the Middle Ages the Macartneys were regularly connected with the monasteries of Scotland, often as lawyers, and records of the name can be found in the annals of Newbattle Abbey in the Lothians and at Sweetheart and Dundrennan Abbeys in Galloway. It was through this connection that Macartney of Auchenleck was able to purchase the lands of that name. George Macartney came from a long line of ancestors bearing that name, strongly associated with the county, several of the most distinguished being buried in the graveyard within the ancient precincts of the Cistercian Abbey of Dundrennan on the scenic Kirkcudbrightshire coast.

Of the three branches of the Macartney family, this narrative concerns the Auchenleck branch, one of whom, bearing the same forename as the subject of this work, settled in Ireland in 1649, and proclaimed William and Mary in Belfast twenty years later, having played a prominent part in establishing the prosperity of that city. Perhaps the most distinguished member of this branch of the family however was Lord Macartney who, among other distinctions, became Governor of Madras in 1781 and subsequently the first Ambassador to China in 1742; an important early family link with that country.

George Macartney's father was Sir Halliday Macartney, who was connected with many of the prominent Galloway families, and continued the association with China by becoming councillor and secretary to the first Chinese legation in London, work which lasted over thirty years beginning in 1877. He returned to retirement at Kenbank near St John's Town of Dalry in Galloway in 1906, and was buried in Dundrennan Abbey, near his boyhood home at Dundrennan House. His strong connection with the area was continued when his eldest son, George, was made a ward of Sir Halliday's old school friend, James Borland of Castle Douglas in the same county, while Halliday was serving in China. To cement this connection, Borland's daughter, Catherina Theodora, who had known George from childhood, married George in 1898.[3]

The question which might arise is why write about events which happened mainly over a century ago, focused on one of the most remote British consular locations in the world: it was said that it flew the only Union Jack between India and the North Pole. Apart from the connection of the main subject in the person of George Macartney and thus bearing at least a remote connection to this author's family, the geographical location of these events is one which still has geopolitical significance today. It lies at the cross-roads of Central Asia, bordered by such turbulent states as Afghanistan, Kashmir, and Tibet, not to mention the break-away territories from the previous Russian hegemony, within which ferocious local wars have broken out. Pan-Islamic movements have developed in Xinjiang in recent years, to China's discomfiture, and the Muslim and Turkic-speaking peoples on that county's extreme western border have become restive.

In some ways, Central Asia has come to be regarded as an extension of the Middle East, with all its religious and political rivalries. (In February 2012 Muslims ran amok killing twelve people near Kashgar, while a previous eruption in 1990 left 107 dead.) The 'Great Game' played out between Russia and Britain in the latter part of the 19th century and the beginning of the 20th has resonances in today's political tensions in this vast area. Not only that, but there is now competition for the invaluable oil and mineral resources of this volatile region. New alignments are now occurring. As Peter Hopkirk writes in his foreword 'The New Great Game' to the most recent edition of *The Great Game* (OUP, 1991): 'For the Kremlin, like the White House, the ultimate nightmare is Muslim fundamentalists armed with weapons of mass destruction using Central Asia as a base for foreign adventures.... [China] has reasons other than trade for building good relations with the new Central Asian republics, notably fears of nationalist uprisings, fuelled and armed from across the border, setting its own Muslim territories ablaze.'

The older title of the 'New Dominion' still describes the relationship accurately, as Xinjiang – a province larger than France, Germany and Britain combined, more than one-sixth of all Chinese territory – had come under more than nominal Chinese control only from the mid-19th century when the population was dominated by Turkic-speaking people, quite distinct from the mass of the Han Chinese elsewhere in the Chinese Empire.

The older 'Great Game' – that reciprocal shadowing of Russian and British spying activities across the Himalayas – has been written about extensively and use has been made of these fascinating narratives where they bear upon Macartney's time and concerns. However, special acknowledgement must be paid to two very different works on the latter. The first is *Macartney at Kashgar* by C.P. Skrine and Pamela Nightingale, the subtitle of which – *'New Light on British, Chinese and*

Russian Activities in Sinkiang, 1890-1918' – is an indication of its serious political emphasis, eschewing in the main the personal life of its central subject. (It was written chiefly from the Political and Secret Records of the India Office which contain Macartney's fortnightly reports from Kashgar: Sir Clarmont Percival Skrine was temporarily Consul at Kashgar in the years 1922-24.)

The second main source is the much lighter, but delightfully anecdotal account by Macartney's wife Catherine, in *An English Lady in Chinese Turkestan,* first published in 1931 (and published in Chinese and Japanese in 1997 and 2007 respectively), which quite properly skirts around the main business in which the Special Agent (and later British Consul) was involved. (Macartney himself wrote nothing of his time as a diplomat *extraordinaire.*) It does however shed light on the difficulties of being a wife and mother in one of the remotest consular areas in the Empire with virtually no contact with other British women and the loneliness of that position, compounded by Catherine's lack of language in her early years at Kashgar. While Britain's diplomatic representative was expected to rise to whatever professional challenges arose in his district, his wife was equally expected to cope with all the household crises which inevitably arose in a situation where the usual domestic support systems were largely absent. (To avoid repetitive references, citations are made to both of these works only where direct quotations are involved.)

Neither of these says much, if anything, about Macartney's archaeological collections or his contribution to the great discoveries of ancient Buddhist culture at Dunhuang, among the most important in the 20th century. This work therefore attempts to bring these different elements of his life together, to provide in a single volume a more rounded picture of the man and his achievements. The present biography is unusual in that it contains barely a single word actually spoken by this notoriously silent man.

CHAPTER ONE

A Chinese Beginning

When Halliday Macartney entered Major Gordon's room on the morning of 7 December 1853, he found the veteran soldier sobbing.[4] Gordon reached under his bed and drew out an object wrapped in a bloody silk scarf, exclaiming: 'Do you see that? Do you see that?'

Unwrapping it, Macartney, at this time commander of Li Hung Chang's Trained Force, fighting the Taiping rebels, stared into the distorted open-mouthed face of one of its most prominent rebel leaders, Lar Wang. Gordon had given a solemn assurance to Lar Wang, that if he surrendered the fort at Soochow with its 40,000 armed rebels, he would not be harmed – but Gordon's Ever Victorious Army had gone on a rampage, killing men, women and children by the hundreds. Gordon burst into hysterical tears in front of Macartney and was totally distraught by what he regarded as an ineradicable stain on his honour.

There remained a real threat to the safety of the women and children of the Wang family. Macartney solved this adroitly by declaring them his personal war loot. In his *Life of Sir Halliday Macartney*, his biographer, Demetrius Boulger, goes to some pains to describe the events which led to the subsequent legal marriage of his subject to Lar Wang's daughter, very much aware of how this might be viewed in the European circles of the time: '...it requires more than ordinary delicacy in treatment. Lar Wang's son Tchin-tang was left with Macartney for his safety and the latter became acquainted with and interested in the family of the late Taeping chief.'[5]

*

In the middle of the following year, Macartney, disguised as a merchant, was able to spy on the remaining Taeping forces still holding the key city of Nanking and to lay down the plan of attack which enabled the Imperial Army to recapture the second city of the Chinese empire, at a cost of 100,000 lives, over three days. Thus he had played a signal part in the ending of a rebellion against the ruling Manchu dynasty which had lasted for twelve years, and by modern estimates resulted in between twenty and seventy million deaths – in terms of numbers, the worst war of modern times. He became responsible for the building and operation of a fully-equipped arsenal at Soochow, and honoured by the Chinese, was convinced that his future life lay in China – he had been in that country since 1860.

Of this juncture in Macartney's life, Boulger writes:

He felt that by taking the usual course in marrying a lady of his own race and religion he would be raising an impediment in his own path...there was really only one alternative before him, and by now speaking fluent Chinese, he knew that to accomplish his aims to secure a senior position, he would require to take up permanent residence in the country.[6]

Boulger goes on to say:

Once he had made up his mind to settle down in the land his thoughts naturally turned to marriage. But if he had married an English or other European lady, however, that would interfere with the realisation of his main plan, which was to gain an ascendancy over the Chinese...Macartney adopted it without probably taking into account all the consequences that would follow...should the scene of his activities ever again be changed from the Celestial Empire to his own country...Macartney voluntarily and of set purpose, had fixed his home and his ambition, not merely in China, but among the Chinese. It was therefore, in strict harmony with his views that he should take unto himself a Chinese wife.'[7]

Reading between the lines, it seems as if Boulger is trying to deflect any implied criticism of his subject in the face of likely opprobrium from his own country-folk for his course of action by suggesting that this association was both logical and convenient.

Macartney decided to marry one of the members of the Wang household under his protection, Lar Wang's attractive daughter, whom he married in December 1864, following all the accepted social customs and laws of the country: this was no mere temporary irregular alliance. As a sister of Lar Wang and therefore coming from a princely family, she has sometimes been described as a 'princess' which is how she was designated in the English press at the time. She was said to be intelligent and of good appearance, but lived strictly apart and did not receive European visitors – she was never presented to Macartney's friends, though, according to one correspondent, this may have been a strict adherence to Chinese family etiquette. Later, Macartney apparently spoke to his cousin and closest confidante, Lady Crichton-Browne, of his Chinese wife and family in terms of warm affection. Letters refer to her by the honourable designation 'tai-tai' or 'lady' of wealth and privilege.

The arsenal was moved to Nanking in 1865, where it was supervised by Macartney for ten years. But in 1875, his appointment was terminated and he returned to England as a member of the first Chinese (Kwoh) Embassy, although it seems to have been his intention to return to China. However two years later, he was appointed Secretary to the first Chinese Mission at the Court of St James and subsequently became secretary and counsellor to the Chinese legation in London, when China was for the first time establishing formal diplomatic relations with the modern 'barbarian' world. He was a trusted emissary and advisor in all important overseas negotiations for that legation for the next thirty years until his death in1906, but never returned to China. Although he left his wife behind, he remained married to her until her death in 1878. They had a daughter and two sons, the elder of whom, George, is the main subject of this work.

George was born on 18 January 1867 in Nanking and would therefore have been ten years old when he returned with his father to England on 21 January 1877, having spent his early formative years in China, no doubt playing with other Chinese children and becoming fluent in the language, while absorbing some of the mores of his birthplace. It may be that his mother held in her heart the thought of the return of her family, after a temporary stay in England, but that hope would have been extinguished when her husband secured a position in London. Her death two years after their departure might well have been hastened by the dismal prospect of never seeing her children again. (Her daughter had been taken by Halliday Macartney to England for schooling on a short visit he made there in late 1873, while he returned to China in the following spring.)

Apart from the culture shock of arriving in a new country, George was subjected to the rigours and formality of an English public school as pupil number 2463 at Dulwich College in London. This was (and is) one of the premier schools in England, and in 1877 was ranked fourth by the Oxford and Cambridge Joint Board after Eton, Rugby and Marlborough, with a particularly impressive record of first class degrees by former pupils from the Oxbridge institutions. Alumni also won several gold medals awarded by the Royal Geographical Society – geography studies seemed to be a school strong point at this time.

The school was fortunate in having as its headmaster the Rev. Dr Alfred Carver who promoted a liberal education, emphasising a broad curriculum, and besides the traditional classics, encouraged science, even going so far as to commission laboratories and workshops. It also had the strong sporting ethos of public schools of the period, but it is difficult to envisage the slightly-built

George, with his extreme modesty and reticence, being enthusiastic about the more physical games and the contemporary cult of 'manliness.' In fact it was said that he hated all sports, but showed that he did not lack physical toughness in his later arduous mountain journeys.

Although he was not apparently particularly oriental in appearance, one can only conjecture his reception by schoolboys who regarded being English as a mark of supreme distinction, and even if they treated others kindly, looked on them as inferiors, when the notion of a dominant Empire was at its apogee. George's quiet nature and disinclination to promote himself or his undoubted talents was frequently remarked upon in later life and may well have been reinforced by the overwhelming experience of public school life in the mid-Victorian era.

Above all, he would be identified as the product of a mixed marriage, a particular taboo of the time, with genetic, racial, and social undercurrents. (Contemporary writings bear ample evidence of attitudes which are not now acceptable.) It is interesting that while Boulger's biography has separate studio photographs of both Halliday's second wife and his family by her, it has none of his first wife or the family she bore him. Nor is there apparently any record of her Chinese name.

It may have been Halliday's subsequent second marriage, after the death of his first wife, to Jeanne, daughter of Jean Leon du Sautoy of Fontainebleau, in 1884, which prompted him to send George to the College of Bernay, in the district of Eure in Normandy and subsequently to Caen University, where he graduated in 1886 as *bachelier des letters* in 1886. However, for those intent on the diplomatic service, profiency in a modern language was obligatory and many candidates went to France or Germany to acquire this.

He would also require proficiency in Latin and a knowledge of the constitutional history of England, according to the 'Regulations for Her Majesty's Diplomatic Service' as confirmed by Earl Granville in

1872.[8] At both Eure and Caen, Macartney would have found a congenial academic and cultural environment, the old town of Bernay particularly, in its atmospheric canals and old rustic houses, providing an insight into European culture, while the even more ancient monuments of Caen introduced him to the long association between England and France. Throughout his time in England and continental Europe, he most frequently spent his holidays with the Borland family, James Borland being an old schoolmate of Halliday Macartney in Castle Douglas, Kircudbrightshire. Perhaps because of Halliday's frequent travels, James Borland was appointed a ward for the young George, who in turn became close to the ship-owner's family.

CHAPTER TWO

Younghusband

In 1887 the young George Macartney (he was only twenty years old), sailed for India. His deepest wish, to serve in a consular position in China, was denied to him. Instead he was assigned to be the Chinese interpreter to the Burma Commission, a lesser service of the government of India. This is unsurprising, since even in the latter half of the 19th century, the aristocracy made up over sixty per cent of the diplomatic service, while in the period 1900 to 1914, sixty-seven per cent were Etonians. (It has been said that the profession of diplomacy was, 'nothing more nor less than a gigantic system of outdoor relief for the aristocracy of Great Britain.') In the 1880s, although the number of Members of Parliament with commercial or industrial backgrounds had risen to 34 percent, only eight per cent of diplomats had this origin. Starting as lowly attachés, such aspiring diplomats were unpaid for the first two years of their careers and would be dependent on parental support of at least £400 per annum. Subsequently, they would receive £150 per annum, according to the regulations of 1874. Promotion was painfully slow, and there were many resignations early in diplomats' careers.[9]

The 'Bible' for diplomatic practice was written by Sir Ernest Satow, whose reference work, as late as 1917, when Macartney was nearing the end of his career, included the following qualifications for diplomats:

> They should have good temper, good health and good looks. Rather above the average in intelligence, though brilliant genius is not necessary. A straightforward character, devoid of selfish ambition. A mind trained by the best study of literature, and by that of history. Capacity to judge of evidence. In short,

the candidate must be a *gentleman*....Science is not necessary, geography beyond elementary notions, is not of great value...some private income, even though the Government may give some special foreign service allowance is very desirable in the lower grades...and the higher the grade, the more of it the better.[10]

The biographer of his subsequent years in Kashgar, C.P. Skrine, summarises the differences that set the half-Chinese Macartney apart from other young men in his profession who formed a caste 'drawn from the cream of the public schools and the universities... [They] went to the East imbued with a sense of national superiority and convinced of their ability and therefore of their right to rule'. [In the early 1950s, in one of the last corners of the fading Empire this had changed little in the experience of the present author.] Products of upper class Victorian society, their 'beliefs in social and cultural superiority and in the divine right of the English people to rule over the coloured races solidified into the rigid code of the Anglo-Indian world; any stepping over the lines of caste and convention was not treated kindly'.[11] Macartney had absorbed that world's eleventh commandment: Thou shalt not marry a native woman; throughout his life he never mentioned his mother – not even, it is said, to his own children.

Macartney apparently never reached Burma. What is known is that soon after his arrival in India he was assigned as an interpreter to what became known as the Sikkim Expedition. This was a not atypical interlude in British imperial history, and exemplifies British attitudes to any constraints on its territorial ambitions and assumed rights to trade anywhere in the world, even in the most remote provinces. Britain became aware of the potential for trade with Tibet from the mid-18th century onwards. In the latter half of the 19th century this possibility focused on the export of Indian tea especially from the new Darjeeling plantations. One difficulty was that the people of Tibet, Bhutan and Sikkim had become accustomed to, and actually preferred, the lower grade 'brick' tea from China, which not unnaturally opposed British trade with Tibet, while the monasteries there did not wish to lose the monopoly they had acquired resulting from their control of the trade routes.

An important consideration for British trade was the development of a road through Sikkim, lying between India and Tibet, which had become a *de facto* protectorate of British India from the time of the East India Company, although historically it had been subject to Tibet and by extension to China. Both these countries feared that through British relations with Nepal, Bhutan and Sikkim, the latter state would become a jumping-off point for encroachment into Tibet. In 1886, the Tibetans attempted to forestall this by sending a small armed force into Sikkim. The British response was to send its own pioneer force to restore the road from Darjeeling to Lingtu in Sikkim which had been effectively closed by the Tibetans and at the same time to give an ultimatum to the Tibetans to withdraw their troops by mid March 1888. Unsurprisingly, the Tibetans ignored this.

Back in London, George Macartney's father, Sir Halliday Macartney, in his capacity as Counsellor to the Chinese Legation, had attempted to explain to the Foreign Office that the Chinese felt that the withdrawal of the Tibetans should be accomplished without resort to force, although they themselves seemed to have little leverage on the Tibetans.[12]

The result was a foregone conclusion, despite the difficulty of the terrain and climate for the British forces. The well-equipped Derbyshire Regiment, supported by artillery, eventually overcame surprisingly stiff Tibetan resistance over several months, culminating in the Anglo-Chinese convention of 1890 which delimited the border between Tibet and Sikkim and ended Tibet's claim to suzerainty over Sikkim. There is no record of the part played by Macartney, but it is interesting to speculate on what, as someone with Chinese blood, he might have thought of this display of *force majeure* against (albeit at one remove) the country of his birth.

What he may not have known was that a young army lieutenant had just completed an epic journey across China, including the Gobi Desert, who was, some thirteen years later, to lead a massive military British invasion into Tibet itself. His name was Francis Younghusband. Despite being only four years older than Macartney, he was to have an important influence on the life and career of the young interpreter.

Francis Edward Younghusband, born in 1863 in India, has been labelled 'the last great imperial adventurer'.[13] He was the epitome of the colonial soldier from a high-ranking military family for whom the term 'muscular Christianity' might have been coined. Despite his background however, he was a misfit in his cavalry regiment, the 1st King's Dragoon Guards, and particularly disliked regimental life, contemptuous of what he saw as the immorality of his brother officers. Having made a considerable early name for himself as an explorer and surveyor, he was able to use his fame to escape from boring cantonment life and 'do his own thing,' establishing a reputation as a hardy adventurer, if something of a 'loose cannon.'

An uncle, Robert Shaw, had been one of the early British planters in Northern India and became secretary of the Kangra Valley Tea Planters Association. In 1868 he had set off for Kashgar in Chinese Turkestan (later to be known as Sinkiang or Xinjiang) to promote the sale of Indian tea, at a time when a Muslim state had just been established there under the military emirate of Ya'qub Beg. Shaw became the first European after Marco Polo to enter the fabled city of Kashgar. There he was put under arrest by the suspicious ruler, but subsequently released to convey messages of good will to the Indian Viceroy, Lord Mayo. He was feted in England as a celebrated explorer and awarded a gold medal by the Royal Geographical Society, later becoming a Political Agent in Yarkand, the commercial centre of Kashgaria. This district covered the southern half of Xinjiang, embracing the great Taklamakan Desert and the encircling oases. Hardly surprisingly, he became an inspiration for the adventurous Younghusband, who, having made the perilous journey across the Gobi, followed in his uncle's footsteps and carried on to Kashgar, arriving there in August 1887.

The city itself lay astride that great east-west trading route, the Silk Road, skirting the deserts of Western China. It had been known since time immemorial not only as a centre for trade and the meeting of merchants, but also as the headquarters for the administration of government for the district of Kashgaria, combining both political and mercantile importance as well as serving as a communications hub. This was undoubtedly the reason it was chosen as the location of the first Russian Consulate in Xinjiang some five years before Younghusband's arrival. It was also to be the diplomatic base and home in this lonely outpost for the first British diplomat in Western China and the subject of this narrative.

It was here that he first met someone who was to dominate young George Macartney's life for many years and to create a crisis for Younghusband himself. That man was Nicolai Petrovsky, appointed in 1882 as the Russian Consul after the signing of the Treaty of St Petersburg. Younghusband's initial impression of the consul was favourable: he proved to be energetic, and given the remoteness of Kashgar, surprisingly knowledgeable about current affairs in the world at large, if suspiciously well-informed about Britain, its Empire and its politics. The young soldier might have been forewarned of Petrovsky's approach to diplomacy when the latter responded to an invitation to tea with Younghusband, accompanied by an escort of sixteen mounted Cossacks bearing the Russian flag. There was to be no doubt about who was boss in the capital of Chinese Turkestan.

As it happened, en route to Kashgar, Younghusband had dined convivially with Captain Bronislav Grombchevsky, another noted explorer in Central Asia, and whom Younghusband considered 'a thorough gentleman' – so much so that, after drinking each other's health in their tented encampment, they were able to discuss objectively the possibility of a Russian invasion of British India. Both were covertly involved in what came to be known as, 'The Great Game', which had become an obsession with both countries from the early 19th century onwards.

Russia had annexed several Central Asian states such as the Khanates of Bokhara, Khiva and Khokand in the first half of that century under the expansionist Tsar Alexander II, but it was its minor encroachment into Afghanistan, which the British considered their province, in the spring of 1885, which set the alarm bells ringing in India. That encroachment was resolved by a redefinition of boundaries and authority, but the relatively low-level clandestine spying which both countries had engaged in become more focused and blatant. (Its first more secret and romantic phase has been colourfully fictionalised in Kipling's *Kim.*)

Thus three great imperial empires – those of China, Russia and Britain – vied for strategic dominance in the contested area north of the Himalayas, where British military presence was weakest. The total annihilation of a whole British expeditionary force in the first Afghan War had brutally exposed that vulnerability. A modern commentator has effectively linked the ancient symbolism of this mountain area with its continuing current strategic significance:

> The Himalayan range is the embodiment of divinity, of nature in its splendour and of culture in the deepest sense of the word. It has been inextricably woven with the life and culture of India since time immemorial…it is the geographical feature that dominates India most and which has acted as a great

natural frontier...the Hindu Kush, Karakoram and Pamir Regions...are continuous and interlocking with the great Himalayan mountain system. Stretching over 2,500 miles from Kashmir in the west to Arunchal Pradesh in the east, it has provided India with a natural and most formidable line of defence. However, its imposing geographical features did not prevent the region from being a complex of cultural interaction, migration, overland trade and communications. The Himalayan region has been the cradle from where ancient Indian culture, including Mahayanan Buddhism spread to different countries...After the Chinese occupation of Tibet, Indian Himalaya became the last refuge of Buddhism....With the disintegration of the erstwhile USSR and the emergence of newly-independent Central Asian states – all having a predominantly Muslim population – a new geopolitical situation has arisen across the north-western Himalayas.'[14]

The main theatre of the spying operations was this mountainous area north of India embracing the Himalayas and the great circle of mountains beyond in Turkestan, with the British especially anxious about preserving this as a buffer zone against further Russian encroachment from the north and west. Anyone travelling in these regions was regarded as a potential source of information, whether as traders, sportsmen, surveyors, scientists or explorers: Younghusband seemed tailor-made for a mission he had proposed in early 1890 to investigate the sixty-mile gap between the Chinese Empire and Afghanistan, known as the Wakhan Corridor; which might be claimed by the Russians. He suggested that he proceed to Kashgar and settle the issue with the Chinese officials there. He was enthusiastic about the prospect, with its overtones of glamour and potential danger – what the Russians described as 'the Tournament of Shadows.' His reputation as an avid explorer provided some sort of cover. What he needed was a competent interpreter in the Chinese language: the choice of George Macartney was to prove especially fortunate.

French says, 'In the racially hierarchial world of British India, Macartney's origins were dealt with by being politely glossed over. Official documents always stress his 'good knowledge of Chinese customs' while ignoring his mixed parentage. French says that Macartney was reticent and withdrawn – a feature noted by several others – and claims that this was 'a result of his enforced double identity'. Younghusband complained that his interpreter tended to approach diplomatic problems from a Chinese point of view. 'Macartney is a good enough fellow in his way but he is not English', he wrote to his sister.[15]

Younghusband and Macartney, with several of the men who had accompanied the explorer on his trans-China expedition, left Simla at the end of June 1890 and proceeded to Leh, in Ladakh – considered the last refuelling station before the long dreary marches across the Karakoram Mountains, a six-hundred mile trek from the plains of India over some of the most barren landscapes in the world. The journey was not without its privations: some nights, at 10,000 feet above sea level on the border of the Pamirs, the temperature fell to minus thirty degrees centigrade, i.e. fifty degrees of frost.

They reached the fertile southern oasis of Yarkand in Chinese Turkestan on the last day of August and Kashgar at the beginning of November, where Younghusband's official duties kept him for the winter. Younghusband had purchased from a Kirghiz a comfortable and highly decorated yurt which he pitched in the garden of a rambling native house on the north side of the old city, allocated to the travellers and known as Chini Bagh ('Chinese Garden') and which was to become Macartney's home for nearly thirty years.

Younghusband was looking forward to renewing his acquaintance with the Russian Consul Nicolai Petrovsky – but he was to receive a rather rude shock.

CHAPTER THREE

The Problem with Petrovsky

After the fall of the Muslim state under Ya'qub Beg some ten years previously, the Chinese had resumed governance of Eastern Turkestan in 1877 under the name, 'The New Dominion'. An elderly Chinese governor was appointed, but exercised little power, while in 1882 the Russians had been allowed to establish a consul there, together with an escort of fifty-five Cossack cavalry. Consul Petrovsky, an able, ostensibly charming and forceful personality, soon established his authority, partly through a system of informants (he even succeeded in gaining access to the Chinese Governor's official communications) and partly through a display of power. He was renowned for being able to switch arbitrarily from genial bonhomie to spiteful aggression as the mood took him: he was acknowledged as a cunning adversary, who skilfully ignored the wishes of his political masters when it suited him, allying himself with the hawks in the Russian military establishment.

Petrovsky would have been well aware that although the British had established reasonably friendly, if informal, relations with the autocratic ruler of East Turkestan and Kashgaria, Ataik Ghazee, through the Forsyth Mission in 1870, the subsequent report by the British agent Ney Elias in 1885-6 struck a very pessimistic note.[16] Petrovsky himself was openly contemptuous of the Chinese, whether as officials or ordinary citizens. Since then there had been no effective British presence in the province. Petrovsky would have smirked at Younghusband's maladroit attempt to impress the Chinese Taotai by promising to remove the Afghans from the Pamirs and to secure Chinese interests there – a promise that was promptly repudiated by the British authorities when the Emir of Afghanistan protested loudly.[17] It did nothing for Britain's reputation with the Chinese that they had established relations with the Muslim usurper, Ya'qub Beg, who had dramatically broken away from Chinese control, nor that Younghusband's uncle had been his messenger to the Indian government.

To complicate matters, the British authorities had ambivalent attitudes, varying between those who favoured a so-called 'forward policy' of active intervention – including the use of military power – to secure British interests, and others who promoted a policy of 'masterly inactivity' to protect the *status quo*. Younghusband would have stood with the former, while Macartney was later to eschew this approach in favour of quiet diplomacy.

Although on the surface Petrovsky appeared hospitable, inviting Younghusband and Macartney to discussions at the rather grand modern Russian consulate in Kashgar, when they talked apparently freely about the local political situation, Petrovsky's superior knowledge and experience quite wrong-footed Younghusband, which was of course exactly what the Russian consul intended. The honest British explorer-cum-spy was quite out of his depth, and with no readily accessible advice on how he should act. Russian agents had covertly followed the British party all the way from India and even now Younghusband's letters to Simla were being intercepted (Younghusband was sufficiently naïve to entrust his mail to Russian couriers) while his communications with the Chinese authorities were well known to the Russians.

Of Petrovosky, Younghusband said, 'He was agreeable enough company in a place where there was no other,' but he cheerfully admitted to lying whenever it suited him and had a complete lack of scruples.[18] He was singularly well-informed and had a network of spies, whose tentacles reached everywhere. Younghusband had instructions to try to persuade the Chinese to send troops into the Pamirs to forestall the Russians, but Petrovsky was later to boast that everything that passed between Younghusband and the Taotai was immediately communicated to him.[19] In this game of cat and mouse, there was no question of which was which. Meanwhile, the unobtrusive but shrewd interpreter would have been quietly absorbing and analysing the various moves on the chessboard.

The young soldier was making no progress on the question which his mission was meant to resolve, that of the Wakhan Corridor in Afghanistan. Together with personal problems (he received news early in the following year that his offer of marriage to an Englishwoman had been rejected, followed shortly by the death of his mother) it is hardly surprising that he felt depressed. He was pleased enough to ride out of the city for India at the end of July1891 after nine frustrating months in Kashgar, which he found uninspiring. With the agreement of the British authorities in India, he left Macartney behind at Chini Bagh to keep an eye on British interests, the sole and unofficial representative of Britain in the whole of central Asia.

Of his travelling companion, Younghusband said:
… we had been together for a year now, and the greater part of the time by ourselves. It does not follow that two men who have never seen each other in their lives before can get on together for a year at a stretch without a break, and with scarcely a change in society. I felt particularly fortunate, therefore in having for a companion a man who was not only a first-rate Chinese scholar, but who was also even-tempered, and willing to give and take, as travellers have to be.. .[20]

Given the differences in their respective backgrounds and personalities, this is both a generous accolade and an indication of Younghusband's judgement in assessing Macartney's qualities. Previously, he had written to his sister Emmie:

'Macartney is not the sort of chap one would choose as a particular pal in civilisation – but he does not bother one and he takes a good deal of interest in things so that we get along very comfortably – going our separate ways during most of the day and meeting at meals.'[21]

When Younghusband returned to India he wrote to the Foreign Secretary, Sir Mortimer Durand:

'...I received very valuable assistance from Macartney, and on one or two occasions I must acknowledge that his more impassive temperament kept me within proper bounds in dealing with the Chinese when their quiet obstructiveness was causing me to lose my self-control. When he has a little experience of working on his own account, I feel sure that you will find him a useful man up there...'

For his part, according to Skrine, Macartney apparently had the greatest admiration for Younghusband and the time he spent in his company was probably the most formative of his life. Macartney's wife Catherine herself commented that her husband never tired of recalling his adventures in the company of the upright imperial soldier.

In the course of a small expedition to Chitral early in 1893, which was commanded by Surgeon-Major George Robertson, accompanied by the Hon. Charlie 'Bruiser' Bruce, Younghusband fantasised about going to Tibet, which apparently appealed to Robertson. The latter suggested that Younghusband should accompany him on a journey to Lhasa with Macartney and Mr Bruce: 'Mr Macartney would go as a Chinaman in charge of a caravan of merchandise. Mr. Robertson would go as his secretary and Mr. Bruce and myself as servants and camel men.'[22] Fortunately this hare-brained scheme came to nothing.

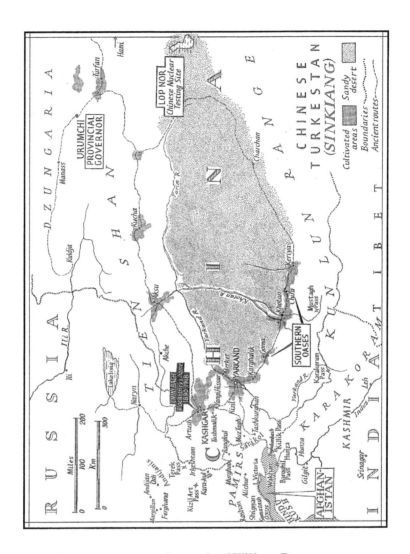

Based on a map drawn by William Borage,
as in, C.P. Skrine & P.M. Nightingale (1973),
Macartney at Kashgar.

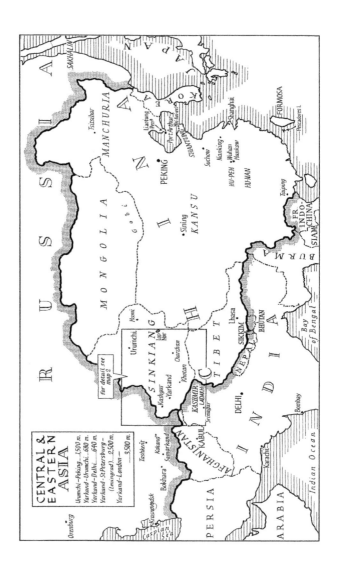

**Based on a map drawn by William Borage,
as in, C.P. Skrine & P.M. Nightingale (1973),
*Macartney at Kashgar.***

CHAPTER FOUR

Xinjiang

Xinjiang is the most westerly and most remote of the Chinese provinces. (*See map,* "Chinese Turkestan" *preceding this chapter*) Previously known as Chinese Turkestan, it is bounded on the north by Siberia, on the west by Russian Turkestan and India, on the south by Tibet, and on the east by Mongolia and the Chinese province of Kansu. (*See map,* "Central Eastern Asia", *preceding this chapter*) It is now administered as the Xinjiang Uyghur Autonomous Region by the People's Republic of China, the name reflecting its mainly Turkic-speaking population. Its 1,664,900 square kilometres, forming one-sixth of China, makes it larger than Great Britain, France, Germany and Spain combined. In Macartney's time, Kashgar was a five month journey from Peking. It is claimed to be the furthest from the sea of any city in the world.

It is largely desert surrounded by high mountains, with the Tien-Shan range and the Pamir Mountains dividing Xinjiang from East Turkestan, which, during the period covered by this work, was part of the Russian empire. The Tien-Shan, or Celestial Mountains, also divide the northern Dzungharia and the southern Kashgaria portions of Xinjiang respectively. The mountain ranges, including the Karakorum, Kunlun and the Hindu Kush to the south, form a series of concentric arcs around the great low-lying Tarim Basin and the feared Taklamakan Desert, the second largest desert on earth.

The outermost of these encircling snow-covered mountains give way to a thin circle of arid foothills and boulder-strewn alluvial fans, before reaching its fringe of fertile oases such as Kashgar, Yarkan and Khotan, all depending on the waters of the Tarim River and its tributaries. Last of all lies the innermost huge centre, a sea of sand dunes, the Taklamakan Desert. By comparison, the archaeological explorer Sir Aurel Stein described the other deserts of the world as 'tame': '...the dunes of the Taklamakan and the wastes of hard salt crust or wind-eroded clay of the Lop desert which stretch almost unbroken for 800 miles from west to east, without any human existence and hardly any animal or plant life thro' lack of moisture. It was notorious for howling demons and black storms of sand and stones which overcame whole caravans, and the dunes rose to 300 ft or more.'[23]

Mildred Cable gives a graphic account of the onset of such a *burhan*, or dry desert storm.

> Before long, there is a distant roar, and a cloud like rolling smoke with a livid edge advances and invades the sky, blotting out sun and daylight; then suddenly the sand-storm breaks on the caravan. No progress is possible and human beings shelter behind a barrage of kneeling camels from the flying stones and choking sand. ...the only safe course is to stay still until it has exhausted itself...[24]

Central Asia was among the most disputed regions in conflicts between empires and ideologies, particularly during the late 19th and the first half of the 20th century, covering exactly the period when George Macartney was attempting to maintain British interests from Kashgar. It was at the crossroads of both war and commerce between Europe and Asia, of special interest to the British imperial rulers of India, with competition for control and influence in the buffer states between the British and Russian empires.

Apart from the nomadic Kirghiz people utilising the higher pastures, the population of Kashgaria is concentrated in the fertile oases around this desert, including the old capital of Kashgar as the centre of government and the much larger commercial centre of

Yarkand to the south. Each town of any size had its own *yamen* or government office which also served as the official residence of the Taoyin,[25] and often as barracks for the predominantly Chinese troops. The cultivated areas round these oases are completely dependent on streams from snow meltwater in the mountains providing for an ancient system of intricate canals, as rainfall everywhere is minimal at only 64 millimetres each year.

It is this dryness – one of the driest cities in the world – which makes the low winter and relatively high summer temperatures bearable, while snow is rare. However, winter temperatures could be as low as minus 13 degrees Celsius, but not infrequently reaching 38 degrees Celsius in midsummer. The climate is thus a comparatively healthy one, although the spring winds from the mountains bring a burden of fine *loess* dust which permeates everything: for visitors this can come as an unwelcome surprise. Catherine, Macartney's wife, describes one such dust storm:

> I saw from my window what looked like a great black pillar advancing towards us through the clear air, with the sun shining on either side of the black mass. It grew bigger and bigger, while the sun became a ball of red before it disappeared entirely. On the other side of the river, the trees were bending, and over us an uncanny stillness hung. The sky grew darker and darker, and then I heard the wind shrieking in the distance and knew from experience that it was time to shut all windows and doors. …with a roar, the storm burst upon us. The trees bent as though they must break and it grew dark as night; while the dust in the air penetrated through the cracks and crevices covering everything, making it difficult even to breathe. The force of the wind was so great that it was well-nigh impossible to stand against it…[26]

Like other oases in the region, the hinterland of Kashgar is famous for its abundant vegetable and fruit production, the many species of flowering fruit trees lining the canals being a noted feature of the early summer. (It has been suggested that the easy abundance of food has contributed to the general lethargy of the population.) The soil is made up of the sandy *loess* blown on the wind, and despite its appearance, is remarkably fertile. Cotton is grown, spun, and woven into cloth for export, in addition to wheat and rice. Mildred Cable gives a description of the Gobi oasis of Tunhwang which verges on the paradisical:

> During the spring the fruit orchards show masses of pear, peach and nectarine blossom; all the fields are green with sprouting corn and every bank is covered with the blue desert iris. A little later, when the fruit blossom has disappeared, the opium poppy bursts into flower, covering a wide acreage as with a veil of gossamer, sometimes shaded from the faintest touch of pink to deep rose, and at other times scarlet streaked with silver-grey. All through the summer, the land yields a succession of crops which include wheat, Indian corn, millet, sorghum, hemp and field peas, with a profusion of vegetables such as aubergines, scarlet capsicum, potatoes, many kinds of beans, carrots, celery onions, leeks, golden pumpkins, and green cucumbers. At different seasons, fields are gay with patches of blue flax, pink buckwheat and yellow colza.[27]

The dominant Turkic people are hospitable and even-tempered: Younghusband described them as having the 'essence of imperturbable mediocrity,' with none of the religious fanaticism of other Muslim communities. However, Skrine remarked that moral and intellectual progress in Kashgaria was absent, and for much of the 20th century, as previously, there was strict censorship of virtually all printed material.[28]

Mildred Cable, after a long association with the desert peoples, had a poor opinion of Turki domestic life:

The men live their own separate life of business friendships and convivialities, in which the women have no part and of which they know next to nothing. In contrast with the highly organised Tungan home, the Turki household has no method at all....the women do a bit of cooking when they feel the need for it...amid the Turkis, all is noise and turmoil...the Turki hostess only stays quiet for a few minutes at a time...the foundation of the Turki home is undisguised gratification of sensuous pleasures. The man comes home to sleep, and all the relationships of the home centre on his use of those hours of darkness. On that score he is master, and tyrannical in his use of power, for the male creature has unquestioned right of dictatorship in the Turki world. He has too many children to be attached to any one of them...[29]

Life revolved round the marketplace, mosques and Sufi shrines, while the Turkis had little contact with the Chinese officials who lived in their own walled town some distance away. Sometimes disputes had to be taken there – on one occasion, in Macartney's time, two rain-makers, well paid for their trouble, were caned and thrown into the Chinese stocks for a too successful demonstration of their powers.

Despite occasional rebellions, in Macartney's time, the Turkic people seemed content to live under the relatively benign Chinese rule, remaining as cultivators and small-time traders, while the pastoral Kirghiz of the mountains had their own distinctive nomadic way of life. The exception to this amicability among the Muslims were the Tungans (or Dungans), war-like Chinese Muslims from Kansu province, who may have been Turkish originally, but had adopted Chinese manners and customs. Mainly located in the north of Xinjiang from the 17th and 18th centuries onwards, they had a reputation for martial ferocity which could affect the balance of power in the province. Corruption was however widespread in both Chinese and Turkic communities, particularly among those who held any power, and it was largely accepted under a system where officials paid for their appointments and recouped their expenses by various forms of extortion.

Law was backed up at least in theory by the presence of Chinese troops, of which some seven to eight thousand were based in Xinjiang. According to most observers, they took their style from their generally indolent civil officials and laid-back officers. Military discipline seemed non-existent and their first consideration was buttressing their own comforts, while their training and effectiveness were regarded as laughable; one visitor commenting that 'officers and men formed a species of happy family party, rather good at gardening.' Many of the units existed only on paper to enable the officers to draw the pay of the fictitious soldiers. Corruption among both military and civil authorities was thus an accepted way of life. Macartney came to know the affable commander General Wang very well, being frequently invited to dinner and returning the compliment.

One notorious but very common system was for individuals to pay large sums of money to secure a low-level post in either the administration or the army, enabling them to be tax collectors and to accrue as much money as possible during the period of their charge, levying the maximum taxes that the local population would accept without insurrection. Some of the worst offenders were Turki officials who were able to disguise their activities from their generally non-Turkic speaking Chinese overlords. Despite everything, and its total lack of democracy or anything approaching equality, the system worked, just so long as the amenable population did not feel they were being treated totally unjustly, and disturbance was kept to a minimum.

In Xinjiang the Chinese usually built their own cities between two and three miles away from the mainly Muslim population, and tended to keep themselves separate from the latter. All communications in the *yamen* were conducted in Chinese and there was insistence on following Chinese procedure and customs in all official business: otherwise they left the rest of the population to their own devices and did not attempt to introduce education or other improvements or to enforce their own religion on them, apart from requiring the appointment of the religious leaders to be confirmed by the Chinese authorities. Generally speaking, the Chinese and the Turkic peoples collaborated to maintain the *status quo* in order to enjoy an agreeably harmonious existence. That included a conspiracy between the local landowners and traders to assist the Chinese in the determination and collection of taxes, of which both took an acceptable percentage.

Col. Francis Younghusband. He thought Macartney "good enough in his way but he is not English". (BLB)

CHAPTER FIVE

A Home in Kashgar

Lying at almost 1500 metres, Kashgar lies at an important junction of the old Silk Road, made famous in the West by the travels of Marco Polo in the late 13th century, and is regarded as the capital of the district known as Kashgaria. It was typical of Central Asian towns, with its low flat-roofed, mud-built, window-less houses and narrow crowded alley-ways, dominated by the Id Kah Mosque, the largest in China: its old town is considered the best preserved Islamic city in Central Asia. It supports a wide variety of peoples, including Kirghiz, Uzbeks, Kazaks, Uyghurs – the dominant Turkic-speaking people – and nowadays an increasing population of Han Chinese.

In Macartney's time, each of the old Uyghur city and the new Chinese city were surrounded by thick, crenelated walls with four massive gates, opened at daybreak and closed at sunset with the blowing of horns and the firing of guns. Outside the walls, wide dry moats were dug. The old Turkic city was a maze of narrow winding streets, usually darkened and shaded by reed mats or awnings, and was especially crowded on market day. Then the centre of the great central square was piled high with colourful fruits of every description, while heavily-loaded donkeys, horses, camels and people mingled and jostled in the muddy alley-ways.

On Fridays, the great mosque was the centre of activity, with the men dressed in their best for this day of prayer. The open marketplace and covered close-packed bazaar was a vibrant gathering ground. Apart from the multi-coloured fruit-stalls and other foodstuffs, there would be tea, hardware, furniture, dyes, medicines and imported Indian or Russian clothes, while there were beggars and sooth-sayers by the town gates and entertainers elsewhere.[30] With a written history stretching back to the first century BC, the ancient trading city of Kashgar has been at the centre of religious and racial competition at least from that time. Struggles between the Turks and Chinese are known from the 7th century, followed by the development of Buddhism from India, with the construction of hundreds of monasteries. (The Chinese have conquered the province five times and been evicted four times.) However, by the 10th century, Islam and the Arab influence from the west had prevailed in Kashgaria, albeit under the authority of the Chinese imperial dynasties which had ruled for over two thousand years. The last of these, the Manchu Quing Dynasty, continued until 1912, when the Chinese Republic was established.

Chini Bagh, Macartney's combined residence and office, was typically flat-roofed and occupied three sides of a courtyard on a single floor outside the north walls of the old city. The walls of sun-dried brick were about two feet thick, effectively insulating the house in both summer and winter, and punctuated on the inside with quaintly shaped niches. It had no windows other than those of oiled paper and skylights. (At one point Petrovsky presented the British agent with a pane of glass but some time later, Macartney felt obliged to return it when their relationship broke down.) It has been described as '...on the edge of a bank above a broad stream, it commanded a panorama of fields and gardens surrounded by low hills and, after a rain had washed its air of light dust-haze, mighty ice-crowned peaks in all their majesty – an old, tumbledown, mud-brick garden house.'[31] When Macartney arrived there in 1890, it had few amenities, but as indicated, a spectacular view of mountains up to eight thousand metres from a celebrated long terrace, from which could be seen the watering of donkeys and horses, besides the stream of noisy people on the nearby road.

The large picturesque garden was on two levels, including a kitchen garden and orchard, which provided an abundance of peaches, apricots, figs, pomegranates, mulberries and vines. To this exotic ambience were added the pets which Macartney acquired, ranging from wolves and a leopard to foxes and stags – at least until the arrival of his wife. To manage this bachelor *ménage* required five private servants, plus three government staff, including two escorts, who wore brilliant red and gold uniforms topped by snowy white turbans, always riding ahead of Macartney. His office had two Indian *munshis* or secretaries, and a Chinese one, together with an invaluable Indian hospital assistant. With their families, the staff made up a small village just outside the main compound.

It was to be his solitary home for the next eight years, but after his marriage to Catherina Theodora it became a 'home from home', not only for the Macartneys, but also for many appreciative travellers in Central Asia. Their appreciation would have been enhanced by one of Macartney's later acquisitions, lugged laboriously over the mountains:

> In the early years of this century Chini-Bagh was distinguished by its lavatory. It was a 'Victory' model with a sturdy mahogany seat, the only flushing thunder-box for two thousand miles. As if this were not enough to secure its place in legend, between its arrival in 1913 and the consulate's demise in 1949, it graced such distinguished bottoms as those of Sir Aurel Stein and Peter Fleming.[32]

Diana Shipton (*The Antique Land*) describes how even as late as the 1940s, the post still depended on runners and riders linking Kashgar with Shrinigar in Northern India, working in relays or groups of three, with the post arriving weekly after a journey of twenty-four days. This was accomplished over snow-covered passes, risking avalanches, crossing rivers swollen by melting ice in summer, along narrow mountain paths. If the mail bags were empty, the disappointment and flatness were acute, since the once-weekly post meant so much. Letters from Peking took two months and parcels five to six months.

Macartney's new home was relatively modest, in marked contrast to that of his Russian counterpart. His apparent lack of formal status and few staff were commented on by several visitors. One of the earliest English travellers to stay at Chini Bagh was Ralph Cobbold who in 1898 was apparently hunting in the Pamirs while on leave from his regiment, although in reality he was spying for the British. He considered the position of Macartney led to ridicule because of his lack of status and authority, emphasised by his being without a uniform and his minimal staff. He was much more impressed by Petrovsky and his Cossack horsemen and admired the Russian strong-arm approach to the Chinese. Being in the 'forward policy' camp, Cobbold thought that the approach of the vacillating British was undoubtedly 'letting the side down'. It was not surprising that he was arrested by Petrovsky as a spy.

CHAPTER SIX

A Precarious Position

One of Macartney's tasks was to support and protect British Indian traders who intermittently sold their goods in the Kashgaria area, risking the long and hazardous journey over the eleven Karakoram passes (only two of them lower than Mont Blanc) via Kashmir and Leh in Ladakh. Obviously such a journey could be justified only by trading in relatively high-value goods such as opium, cotton, piece-goods, spices and hardware and returning to India with marijuana, China tea, silk carpets, gold and silver. Many of the richer merchants had land and property in the province and had married Turkic women, but all hung on to their British nationality, mainly for its protection and consular access for the resolution of disputes with other nationalities. In negotiations, Macartney might use English, Chinese, Turki, Persian, Urdu, and Russian.

Apart from the costs and inevitable losses of the hazardous journey from India, they faced severe competition from the Russians who had secured a favourable treaty from the Chinese for their goods from 1851 onwards, quite apart from the geographical advantages of their proximity to markets in Xinjiang. (By 1900, the extension of the road and railways by the Russians had halved the price of transport of Russian-made goods compared to the costs borne by Indian traders.) This situation was upset by the 1868 Muslim revolt under Ya'qub Beg, who made overtures to the British authorities, dangling the prospect of enhanced trading rights, while curtailing those of the Russians.

Unfortunately, by 1872 Ya'qub Beg could no longer resist Russian military threats to his power and he was forced to concede even further commercial treaties to them, together with a lowering of import duties on Russian goods, and the right to establish agents in any towns in Kashgaria. This was the stimulus for the Forsyth Mission referred to above, to seek comparable privileges, but eventually without success. Not only that, but this alignment with a rebel overlord did not enhance Britain's reputation in the eyes of the Chinese, resulting in the failure of Ney Elias's overtures in 1885 and in their cool reception to Younghusband who had been compromised by his uncle's earlier association with Ya'qub Beg.

Together with Petrovsky's machinations to undermine any British attempts at *rapprochement*, Macartney had been handed something of a poisoned chalice. Neither was his position helped by Chinese resentment in a dispute with the British over Burma, or the earlier incursion into Sikkim. He was however to achieve a singular success much later, in abolishing one high-value item of trade – in securing the freedom of British Indian slaves in Kashgaria.

That satisfaction was to come in the future. What the twenty-four-year-old interpreter, with no previous experience of diplomacy, had to face immediately were considerable challenges, both professional and personal. In the face of Chinese indifference on the one hand and the potential intimidation of Petrovsky on the other, he had to establish his authority as the British representative and a reputation for scrupulousness and firmness in his dealings with both, against a background of minimal resources. As Skrine puts it: '... there could be little hope of challenging the political or commercial domination of Russia.'[33]

On the one hand, Macartney had the enormous advantage of speaking Chinese fluently (which Petrovsky did not) but on the other, his opponent was a master of switching from charming affability to vengeful spite. Further, Petrovsky had behind him a government which regarded Xinjiang as its territory, with a substantial military power to back it, and the Russian Governor-General – also responsible for policy on Kashgar – took his instructions form the War Minister and the Tsar, and not the Russian Foreign Office, which might have preferred the diplomatic approach. The Russian Consul was not slow to compare his own powers and lack of interference from above with the restrictions on British officials reporting distantly either to Calcutta or London.

In similar vein, Petrovsky boasted that the Chinese, in the person of the Taotai, would do exactly as he, the Russian consul, ordered, under threat of a whipping if necessary, or – in the unlikely event of the Taotai's being obdurate – pressure on the Peking Government by the Russians in St Petersburg would soon make them see sense. Hardly surprisingly, Petrovsky regarded the lighter touch of the British in India as being both incomprehensible and weak. It is not surprising that the Chinese were terrified of him. During Younghusband's stay in Kashgar, both he and Macartney were invited to long social evenings with the Russian consul, during which he expanded frankly on the political situation, always with the underlying intention of impressing his British guests with Russian influence and power and his ability to thwart any moves Britain might consider making to restrain this.

The particular personal challenge for Macartney after Younghusband's departure in the summer of 1891 was loneliness. Until the arrival in 1894 of two Swedish missionary families, he was on his own, with no one of his culture to confide in or socialise with, and this was exacerbated by his own extreme reticence and self-containment. That loneliness was assuaged somewhat by the warm companionship of a distinctly eccentric individual whose tattered windblown black cloak and disreputable battered clerical hat were a distinctive feature of Kashgar, scurrying round the town apparently on urgent business.

This was the elderly Father Hendriks who had disagreed with his original Roman Catholic Church and – after much travelling in the Far East – had settled in

Kashgar. He was penniless, surviving on ten to twelve rupees a month in a hovel, and seemed to live on scraps provided by others – mainly bread and vegetables. He was nevertheless cheerful, sociable, and kindly regarded by the inhabitants of the town – all the visitors to Kashgar commented on this unusual man who could speak several languages, was more than competent in geology and astronomy, and loved good conversation.

The exception in this regard was Petrovsky, who exhibited a particular malevolence towards the priest and tried to get him removed – eventually successfully – from his run-down home, possibly because he felt that Father Hendriks' cleverness effectively – though unintentionally – competed with his own. The Russian consul was not above spreading malicious gossip about the innocuous priest. He may also have known that the Dutchman, from his ramblings in the town, knew everything that was going on. The Macartneys called him 'The Newspaper' for his continual exchange of information with all and sundry, and he was to prove a valuable informant for Macartney. It may also have been because of his friendship with the agent, who frequently asked him to join him for meals. The protein provided was apparently greatly appreciated by Hendriks, who claimed, unsurprisingly, that he felt quite different after a dish of meat. It presents an intriguing picture of the dapper half Scot, half Chinese diplomat sitting down to a meal in a remote Central Asian town with a derelict and emaciated ecclesiastical hobo discussing the affairs of the world in their variety of common languages, including Latin. The old priest died of throat cancer in his hovel in 1906, declining the Macartneys' invitation to spend his last days amid the relative comforts of Chini Bagh.

Macartney seems to have been in the habit of giving succour to waifs and strays. A clerk named Wang had been removed from his work at the local *yamen* and was destitute. When Macartney found out his situation and also that he had a considerable interest in Chinese poetry and literature, he invited Wang each afternoon to call at Chini Bagh, where in the garden they would stroll and discuss all aspects of Chinese philosophy and culture, aided by a large Chinese dictionary, with plays, and writings laid out on the garden bench: Macartney was apparently a keen scholar of Chinese literature.

One traveller, David Fraser, paints a charming picture of a frequent scene (with accompanying photo of Macartney in his typical linen suit and Panama hat): 'They walk under the trees and placidly discuss upon philosophy and its bearing upon life, upon theology and its relation to love and being.' Their discussions were helped by hot tea and sizeable portions of afternoon cake, to which Wang was very partial.[34] Many visitors remarked on Macartney's linguistic abilities – apart from English, he spoke fluent French and Chinese, had some German and Russian, and later added Persian, Hindustani and Turkic (a Turkish dialect). This capacity would not have endeared him to Petrovsky, who like most of his consular staff, spoke no Chinese.

The same author was very complimentary about Macartney's resolution of cases involving Indian traders and others. Macartney spent considerable time on tour of his area, working closely with the District Magistrates (*Aqsaquals*) staying in each township for up to a fortnight, where he was usually treated most hospitably. When one trader complained to him over being over-taxed under the foreign goods system, Macartney investigated this promptly to find that there was no fixed rate of tax, which resulted in the singular triumph of having all taxes removed from such goods. Captain Deasy records how Macartney resolved an unpaid debt issue by seizing the ponies of the debtor and handing these over to the creditor. Frazer also praised Macartney's prompt justice, whether by physical punishment, fine or dismissal more or less on the spot, which was immediately accepted simply because of the trust reposed in the British agent and his reputation for fairness.[35]

Fraser went on to say:

Our happy relationships with the Chinese in this part of the world are due greatly to our agent, who has built up for himself a strong position. British prestige has been well maintained. Macartney's knowledge of Chinese language and character have enabled him to maintain personal relationships at times of official stress, thereby tiding over difficulties that might have had unpleasant consequences.[36]

An indication of Macartney's standing was recorded by the *Dumfries and Galloway Standard* of June 1906 when he paid an official visit to Yarkand: 'About 15 miles out, tents were pitched, all the different nationalities turned out to greet the Consul, including Cashmiris, Afghans, Hindoos, Chinese, etc. Five Chinese Ambans also welcomed him, and Macartney rode through the city attended by about 1,000 horsemen.'

As an example of Macartney's firmness and determination, Fraser recalls how, when one owner (at the instigation of the Russian consul) wanted to get rid of his Hindu tenants by hanging the bloody skin of a cow over the entrance to their quarters, the local Chinese authorities resisted Macartney's remonstrations until he took the matter to the Governor, spelling out the situation in no uncertain terms: the skins were removed, despite the presence of an angry mob. It was an important victory in the battle to maintain British authority both with the Indian traders and the Chinese.[37]

Much of Macartney's time was taken up with land and trade disputes around the Northern Frontier, with bewildering (and nowadays often archaic) terms for geographical areas, peoples, languages and allegiances. Hunza was the most northerly princely state in what is now West Pakistan, covering a sub-range of the Karakorams, also known as Kanjut, while Sarikol (Sariquol), with its capital at Tashkurghan, was a border district of the Pamir Mountains, and a meeting point of the four main mountain systems of Central Asia, primarily the Hindu Kush and Himalayas, separating Xinjiang and the Pamir Region from India. The population of about 7,000 were mainly Tajiks, sometimes known as Sarkolis. Around the turn of the 19th century, there were constant disputes between these groups over the rights to cultivation in the Raskam Valley to the north of Hunza proper, disputes which Russia exploited. (The State of Hunza was abolished in 1974.)

It would be tedious to detail the various intrigues and probings stimulated by the Russians from the early 1880s onwards along the contested frontier involving the districts of Chitral, Kashmir, Nagar, Hunza – the last paying formal tribute to the Emperor of China. Hunza was of great strategic importance in commanding, with Nagar, the immediate southern approaches to the main passes linking India with Xinjiang and therefore pivotal to the protection of British India. It was this association with China, and the position of Hunza regarding possible intrusion there by the Russians that prompted the British to exert their authority over the villainous Mir of Hunza, Safdur Ali (he had murdered his father and younger brother to eliminate the competition) in a British military coup in 1891, followed by their installation of a more amenable Mir, Nazim Khan. That episode was to precipitate a crisis for Macartney in his relations with the Chinese in particular.

In all of this, the vulnerability and impermanence of Macartney's position was pivotal. In fact, he had no official position and was certainly not regarded as a consul, nor did he receive anything like adequate guidance from the British government in India, which almost certainly did not know what to do with him. He was variously described as an 'agent' or 'assistant' to the nearest British resident, some 650 miles away in Kashmir, through whom all official communications were sent and received. This was reachable only by couriers over passes which were sometimes blocked by snow or floods for weeks at a time. His territory covered some 460,000 square miles, one of the largest consular districts in the British Empire.

Officially, he was still only a lowly member of the Burma Commission. The lack of recognition of his status was of course highlighted by the relative modesty of his quarters and staffing, not least by the Chinese authorities who expected officials to display a degree of pomp and ceremony. The contrast with the Russian consul's ménage could not have been more obvious.

However, Macartney was shortly to add a distinctive feather to his cap. In his conversations with the Taotai over Hunza he had taken the opportunity to raise the question of slaves who were British subjects – the results of raids by Hunza tribesmen along the trade routes leading to Kashgaria. There were considerable numbers of Indian traders, mainly Hindu, in Xinjiang, and a cadre of money-lenders, who were generally despised. Macartney started in a modest way by asking the Taotai's help in securing the release of seven men from Gilgit, and their repatriation if they so wished. The Taotai agreed that this slavery was against Chinese law, but asked that an indemnity be paid to their 'owners' which Macartney was determined not to do.

Despite a suggestion that the Taotai, Macartney and the local Amban ransom the slaves, the British agent stuck to his guns as a matter of principle.[38] Although at this stage the matter was taken no further, Macartney reported that he had hopes for the slaves' eventual release. By February 1892, by sheer persistence, this was achieved. But Macartney had his eye on the remaining five hundred or so slaves in Kashgaria and persuaded the Indian Foreign Secretary to lend his support. After some foot-shuffling, the Taotai agreed to the official British request for an enquiry into the slavery situation, but it took till 1897 before the authorities issued an official proclamation against the keeping of slaves.

The practice was declared to be unlawful, not only in Kashgar, but in all the other towns in Kashgaria, and applied to everyone and with complete cooperation from the Chinese on the matter from then on. Eventually, the provincial Governor ordered that all persons of foreign origins should be offered the chance of freedom, and none would be forced, as a result of having been freed, to leave the country. It was a singular triumph for Macartney, who had been the prime mover, although nothing on this was reported in the British press at the time.

The stance of the Foreign Office and therefore of the Diplomatic Service had changed significantly since Lord Palmerston's time with its robust defence of British interests. In his life of the Minister to China (1865-1870), Sir Rutherford Alcock, Michie claims that there was a sea change in the whole approach to diplomacy, with energy and aspiration being replaced by 'keeping one's nose clean.'

> Ambition was starved among those who had to bear the burden and heat of thirty years residence in China, when they saw good posts thrown away upon men imported for two or three years, who were almost useless...

Michie quotes a veteran member of the consular staff in Peking as saying: 'Would it not be very advantageous if the working hands in the legation were chosen from the most competent Chinese scholars in the consular service?'

This would of course have applied to Macartney.

Michie bemoans the fact that 'notwithstanding their initial qualification, their social standing, and their great opportunities...the number of men of distinction who have emerged from the consular service during the last fifty years seems disproportionately small.' He is talking of the period 1850-1900, regarding the late 1860s as a high point in British consular achievement, particularly in enforcing treaty obligations and defence of trading interests, describing the Foreign Office as subsequently becoming 'invertebrate'.

He is scathing about a British policy of keeping the peace at all costs in China, a policy of which Macartney would have been well aware. Michie derides the fact that 'diplomatic and consular establishments went on grinding out routine despatches and publishing statistical reports but with the tacit understanding that whatsoever is more than these cometh of evil.' His remarks are mainly addressed to the Ministerial legations in Peking, and do not reflect the actual hands-on and day-to-day initiatives of isolated agents such as Macartney, but he was undoubtedly affected by such attitudes. Michie is particularly critical of the impotence of the Foreign Office in influencing the disaster that overtook China in the Sino-Japanese War of 1894 which resulted in the loss of Korea from the Chinese Empire.[39]

View of Kashgar and the Range of Mountains which Divides it from the Russian Possessions, 1868. (Robert Shaw, *Visits to High Tartary*, 1871.)

CHAPTER SEVEN

Hiatus in Hunza

The situation in Hunza was complex, further complicated by traditional slave raiding on the part of the inhabitants. The British government had made it clear that they were prepared to use military force to ensure that Hunza and Nagar remained part of India in the face of the Mir, Safdur Ali's request to China for arms to defend itself from incursions by 'foreigners' – in this case the British. This came to Macartney's notice only via his Persian personal secretary, Abdul Rhaman, who obtained sight of the Mir's letter to the Taotai at Kashgar. Instead of acceding to the Mir's request, the Chinese proposed building a house in Hunza near the frontier and to install a Chinese official there to represent their government's authority and to demand the sight of a Chinese passport on anyone seeking entry to the state. In the hope that he would be supported by the Chinese and the Russians, Safdur Ali ignored the British ultimatum and a campaign ensued which saw the fall of the previously impregnable fort at Nilt to an heroic British attack.

At Kashgar, Macartney knew nothing of this action until the news was brought to him by a merchant named Muhammed Azim Boy, a British protected subject, who had been obliged to act as one of Petrovsky's informants under the shadow of a large debt hanging over his head and under pressure from the Russian consul. Macartney knew immediately, with his own government invading what the Chinese considered their territory, that his decidedly unofficial position at Kashgar was under real threat, while Petrovsky had already labelled him as a British spy. What happened next could have come straight from the pages of an espionage thriller.

When the news was brought to Macartney at Chini Bagh, the merchant was with the Hunza delegation seeking Russian and Chinese help in their war with the British, which information he relayed to Macartney. Two hours later, he returned to Chini Bagh with letters bound in red linen which he claimed had been given to him by the Hunza envoys to deliver to the Russian consul, as Muhammed Azim Boy was known to be a Russian agent, and they did not wish to arouse Chinese suspicions by being seen in daylight to visit the Russian consulate. Macartney was in a serious quandary. This could well be a trap set by Petrovsky to confirm to all that he, Macartney, was indeed a spy, which would justify his expulsion from Kashgar. Macartney was still unsure of the merchant's true allegiance but was sorely tempted. In the end he decided not to examine the letters and was well repaid for his caution.

One of the letters was to Petrovsky himself which he opened in the presence of Muhammed Azim Boy: unfortunately for the Consul the letter was in Persian which Petrovsky did not understand. The merchant translated for him – and repeated the contents verbally to Macartney. Not only was it an appeal from the Mir for help, but complained that the Russians had not built the fort they had promised, while the British army was at his door. Macartney immediately sent a report to Sir Mortimer Durand, Foreign Secretary of the Government of India in late December 1891.

He was still not sure which side Mohammed Azim Boy was on, but on the following day, the merchant reported that one of the Hunza envoys had visited Petrovsky, when the Russian Consul asked him to seek immediate Chinese help, Macartney was convinced that Mohammed was an ally, especially when he was able to relay to the British Consul the terms of the British ultimatum to the Mir. After a discussion with the cautious Chinese Taotai, Macartney was convinced that the Chinese would do very little if anything to help the Mir. The issue was resolved when the British overwhelmed the Hunzas by taking their last defensible fort and the Mir fled north into Chinese territory, whereupon the British annexed both Nagar and Hunza. Macartney had contributed significantly to reducing the potential hostility of the Chinese to the Hunza question which would otherwise have increased the leverage of the Russians.

Macartney had won his spurs in a most fraught situation which would certainly have tested the diplomacy of a much more experienced official, but he had also quite clearly gained the confidence of the Taotai, greatly aided by his command of the language. But he was not out of the wood yet. Up to this point, possibly with their eye on the Hunza problem, the Chinese had done virtually nothing to prevent a Russian incursion into the Pamirs. On his return from Kashgar, Younghusband had shadowed a group of Cossacks under Colonel Yonoff, who felt obliged to expel him, albeit very courteously, claiming ominously that the Pamirs were now Russian territory.

To all of this, the Chinese had characteristically turned a Nelson eye, but Macartney was acutely aware, despite Russian subsequent disavowal of Yonoff's actions, of the threat in the Pamirs, which the Chinese were in no position to defend. Fortunately, and despite the British invasion of Hunza, the provincial government at Urumchi (Urumqui) was more alert to the danger and sent 200 cavalry into the disputed area to make their point. But the territorial game of chess was by no means over.

Storm clouds were still brewing, with reports of Russian troop movements: no less than 3,000 Cossacks with sixteen guns were being assembled at Osh, and by February 1892, there were rumours of an invasion of Hunza. Petrovsky increased his surveillance of the young British agent, so that he was shadowed wherever he went; Petrovsky was particularly suspicious of his friendship with the informative Father Hendriks. Meanwhile, the Chinese military command was instructed to defend Chinese territory against either the Russians or the British.

Among the British authorities, there was a definite opinion that the Russians intended to annex the Pamirs in the near future, a view shared by Macartney.

By early spring, with the advance of 300 Russians into the Pamirs, the Chinese and the Russians appeared to be on a collision course, all of which Macartney reported. He also reported the prospect of revolution in Kashgaria by the disaffected Turki population, if the Chinese were defeated, and with the possibility of the Kirghiz pillaging the towns, all of which would be music to the ears of the Russians. The whole issue collapsed with the end of an unusual spell of mild weather to be replaced by heavy snow storms, precipitating a Russian retreat from the Pamirs. Meantime, Macartney had persuaded the British authorities to adopt a mollifying line towards the Chinese with regard to their suzerainty over Hunza, with the hope that the Chinese in turn might be persuaded to offer a trade agreement and official representation at Kashgar. The sticking point was that the British refused to recognise any Chinese authority south of the Hindu Kush.

There was as a result a temporary freezing of relations, but the British recognition of a Chinese nomination of a new Mir of Hunza restored the all-important face of the Chinese. However, with the ever-present threat from the Afghans, they seemed inclined to settle the vexed Pamir question with the Russians by diplomacy. But at the end of May 1893, the Afghan garrison at Somatash had been reinforced by a further two hundred troops, and the Russian diplomatic offensive broke down when the Chinese refused to concede Somatash and the Alichur Pamir. Meanwhile the Russians were massing their forces along the Pamir boundaries, while Macartney relayed the news of the assemblage of large Russian forces at Osh. By midsummer, all the indications were that the frightened Chinese were prepared to do an about-face and allow the Russians into the Pamirs, while Macartney could get no sensible indications of Chinese policy from the Taotai at Kashgar.

Macartney was faced with the humiliation of seeing all his hopes of stiffening Chinese resolve against the Russian encroachment disappear: his political aspirations were ruined. But he was determined to salvage something from the wreckage of British prestige and by a series of cunning blandishments, succeeded in getting the Taotai to accept a dinner invitation in the face of Russian displeasure, particularly in the person of Petrovsky, of whom the Taotai lived in mortal fear. Macartney would not take 'no' for an answer, but applied pressure in the most diplomatic 'Chinese' way and thus regained some status for his position in Kashgar. Although it might seem a minor matter, it was a reflection of Macartney's sensitive understanding of the importance of appearances to the Chinese mind and his adroitness in reading this. For their part, it is doubtful if the British government fully appreciated, if at all, the value of their unofficial agent in Central Asia.

However, that same government was deeply concerned when it heard that, in July, the Russians had arrived in the Pamirs in force, under Colonel Yonoff, and in a confrontation near Somatash, the Russians had killed a number of Afghans who had refused to recognise Russia's authority over what they considered to be their territory. This had taken place, despite the Russians' assurance that they had no hostile intentions toward the Afghans. One consequence of this, which greatly alarmed the British authorities, was that the Amir of Afghanistan indicated that he intended to withdraw from the Wakhan area, which, as indicated previously, contained the vulnerable gap between the Chinese and Russian disputed area extending to 100 miles of unprotected land, with no other effective British presence there. Meanwhile, the Russians roamed over the Pamirs without let or hindrance, even destroying a Chinese fort and disarming the soldiers stationed there.

Macartney felt peculiarly impotent to influence these momentous events threatening India's northern security, without even the ability to report them to his superiors.

This was made all the more galling because, despite his friendship with the Chinese and his understanding of them, they were effectively broken reeds in the face of Russian power. He must have wondered about his own usefulness as British representative in Kashgar. His thoughts on his journey to Hunza in the company of General Chang would have been gloomy. Acting as interpreter for Chang, he was effective in establishing friendly relations between him and the British at Gilgit, but the General nevertheless reminded them of China's rights over Hunza. At the same time, Macartney took the opportunity of writing to the government of India about his own status and his remuneration, which had not altered since he had first arrived at Kashgar. He emphasised that in Chinese eyes, undue parsimony was not a virtue. Writing on 16 August, 1893, he said:

> The delicacy and difficulties, the isolation and consequent unpleasantness of my position in Chinese Turkestan are not perhaps unknown to you, and I venture to hope that government will consider these inconveniences as grounds entitling me to generous treatment, especially as I have been so long in Kashgar, and there is reason to believe I shall remain here for a further period of indefinite duration.[40]

In the next month he was to make the valid point that, after paying the rent on his house and the salaries of his various assistants and essential couriers, he was left with less than 100 rupees with which to offset political expenses, such as paying informants. Further, he made a request to be transferred from the Burma Commission to the Foreign Department of the Government of India, claiming truthfully that he had not set foot in Burma:

> My work too, in the event of my request being granted, would considerably increase in interest to me, for I should then feel I was serving my own department and not one, as at present is the case,

which is bound to me merely by its own temporary convenience and interests.[41]

This was quite audacious on Macartney's part, reflecting an increased confidence in his own contribution to British interests in his remote outpost, not least in the face of formidable opposition by Petrovsky and the vacillation of the Chinese. He had, in a most delicate situation, played a valuable part in reconciling the Chinese to the British invasion of Hunza, particularly by the relationship he had established with the Taotai. His success in securing the right of repatriation for the British subjects held in slavery in Xjiang – importantly overcoming the issue of compensation – was outstanding. It is difficult not to feel that bureaucratic indolence, possibly coupled with a cavalier attitude towards those on the fringes of the imperial establishment, had led to a convenient neglect of officials such as Macartney in the furthermost outposts of Empire.

Skrine, who had professional consular experience commented:

> It was true that he had failed in the first object of his mission; he had not succeeded in persuading the Chinese to defend their claims on the Pamirs. But he could hardly expect success when the British government could do no better in Peking.[42]

Macartney knew that the recent advance into the Pamirs had increased the importance of the post at Kashgar. Surgeon-Major Robertson, the acting British Agent at Gilgit, paid tribute to his unrivalled knowledge and to 'his dispassionate methods of reasoning, his quiet careful habits of observation, and his experienced tact in dealing with Chinese officials.'[43]

Notwithstanding this, Macartney was understandably disturbed about his reception in Kashgar in the autumn of 1893. It was clear that, despite his good relations with the Chinese, his unrecognised official position had not changed, while Petrovsky continued unabated with his intrigues to discredit him. In his absence, the Russians had been, according to the Taotai, as difficult as ever. However, as a result of his submissions, Macartney did at least receive a significant increase in pay and allowances. What was less satisfactory was the Chinese withdrawal of its troops from their border district of Sarikol in the Pamirs, which the Russians appeared to be claiming, and which was confirmed by Lord Dunmore in conversation with them in the course of his independent travels in the area. The Russians had heard of a forthcoming boundary commission between the interested powers and intended to steal a march on the outcome, with Petrovsky stating to Dunmore that Russia had as much right as China to the Sarikol district.

By this time, Macartney and Petrovsky were not on speaking terms and Dunmore, who was Macartney's guest, was asked by the latter to seek a reconciliation, which was not successful. Petrovsky's comment was significant in its contempt, insisting that Macartney had no credentials or official standing, and dismissed the subject by saying: 'I don't know him as a British official. I once knew him as Younghusband's interpreter, and now I only know him as an English spy.'[44]

Amidst all the claims and counter claims as to rights of territory between the Chinese, the Russians, the Afghans and the British, an Anglo-Russian boundary commission was being proposed, but Macartney was unimpressed. He had been on the receiving end of a dispute about some arms which he had received for his own use and two rifles and two revolvers which were intended as presents for the Chinese envoys who had attended the recent installation of the new Mir of Hunza. Petrovsky made great play of this, eventually writing to the Provincial Governor about the import of arms into Chinese Turkestan, and accusing the Kashgar Taotai of negligence in allowing this. It was typical of a stream of petty annoyances designed to undermine both Macartney and his relations with the Chinese authorities.

The substantial Russian troop movements on the frontier merely served to increase the tension, focused on both the Chinese and Russian attempts to seize each other's couriers: on 14 July, a report by Macartney on the movement of Russian troops was seized by four mounted men, presumably Russian agents. It became a propaganda war, even to the extent of the Russian consul accusing Macartney of abetting his Cossacks in selling property belonging to the Russian government. More importantly, as a result of Petrovsky's machinations, a query was received by no less than the Governor at the provincial capital of Urumchi as to why Macartney should have any official right to transact business on behalf of British subjects, despite his awkward title of 'Special Assistant to the Resident in Kashmir for Chinese Affairs'.

The fuse was lit when a Cossack officer and two other Russians, sightseeing in the garden of a shrine outside Kashgar, were assaulted and injured by a Chinese mob, which the Chinese authorities refused to act on. It was the perfect excuse for the Russians to send their troops into Kashgar. Meanwhile, trouble was also brewing over Russian threats to Afghanistan, which obliged the Amir there to agree to a British proposal in 1893 that he accept suzerainty over the long-disputed Wakhan Corridor, in return for a British promise to support him against any Russian invasion. The dispute over the incident concerning the assault of the Russian officers, despite Petrovsky's demand for satisfaction, petered out, while relations between the Chinese Taotai and Macartney improved perceptibly.

Even Petrovsky offered an olive branch to the British agent, no doubt helped by the threat from a new quarter: Japan. The Japanese in 1894 had inflicted a series of defeats on a weak Chinese army in Korea and Manchuria, and the Russians became worried that it could do the same to them in the far east of their empire. They did not want to be distracted by frontier disputes in the Pamirs, preferring to pursue their trading interests in Xinjiang. The upshot of all this was that in spring 1895, the Pamir Agreement was signed between Britain and Russia regarding the frontier, but left an agreement with the Chinese to be settled by a Boundary Commission, under the leadership of the Surveyor, Col. Holditch, with Macartney acting as assistant whenever required. The Commission set off for the Pamirs in June 1895, with a baggage train extending for 14 miles, and Macartney left on 16 July to join them.

At this point, Macartney took the opportunity to summarise for the British Government his views on the situation in Kashgaria. His conclusion, in the face of Chinese weakness and decline in its empire, was that the Russians were preparing to annex that territory and that Britain should face the reality of having to negotiate an intermediate neutral state between the Russian presence and British India. Meanwhile the work of the Boundary Commission went ahead, and Macartney played an important part in convincing the head of the Commission, General Sir Montagu Gerard, in the course of an eighty-mile reconnaissance of the Taghdumbash Pamir, that the area was effectively occupied and patrolled by the Chinese, against Russian claims over this territory. Macartney had expertly organised the provisioning of the Commission and Gerard was impressed not only by this but also his general ability:

> He is so silent and reticent that he was nearly a month in our camp before I learned that he is a graduate of a French college. You will not easily find another man who knows perfectly Chinese, French, Turki, Persian, Hindustani and English; while his silence and reserve seem to mark him as a very safe Agent indeed in any situation. He is so sober I fancy he drinks about two glasses of wine a week, and he is a perfectly mannered and quiet gentleman.[45]

One of the most contested areas between India and China is Aksai Chin, a high-altitude desert at an elevation of 5,000 metres, with the Karakorum Range forming the *de facto* border between Aksai Chin and the now Indian-controlled Kashmir. At the time of the survey, Britain was primarily concerned that this area did not fall into Russian hands, and Britain proposed a boundary which placed this in Chinese territory, along a line suggested by Macartney. This was presented to the Chinese by Sir Claude Macdonald, the hero of the later siege of Peking during the Boxer Rebellion. The Chinese did not respond to his Note. The British took this as acquiescence. (The Macartney-Macdonald Line is approximately the same as the current Line of Actual Control. China National Highway 219 connects Tibet and Xinjiang, the two strategic Autonomous Regions now administered by China.)

At the end of July, Macartney left for leave in England for the first time in five years. In India he took the opportunity of reminding his superiors of the official British situation in Kashgar, made even more vulnerable by Petrovsky's elevation to Consul-General there, in contrast with his own indeterminate position. Despite General Sir Montagu Gerard's support, he was unsuccessful, with the authorities refusing even to put him on the graded list of the Political Department, on the grounds that Kashgar was the only post where his experience and abilities could be useful – a quite extraordinary lapse of judgement. He remained therefore an outsider with no recognised position or indeed security. Despite this, Skrine says:

> For four years he had shown that not only could he live happily in a remote, inaccessible country with no other Englishman to give advice or companionship, but he had proved himself capable of dealing with the unscrupulous schemes of Petrovsky and the deviousness and vacillations of the Chinese. Unsupported by his own government and pitted against opponents who held all the cards in their

hands, he had survived to return again to Kashgar for another round.[46]

**Kashgar Road Scene showing different modes of
transport on the Silk Road.
Sketch by T.E. Gordon, 1870.
(Wikimedia)**

CHAPTER EIGHT

The Bear Calls the Tune

Soon after his return to England, Macartney went to the home of the Borlands, who, especially during his school holidays from Dulwich College, had provided a warm home-from-home where he was always welcome, because of his father's friendship with James Borland dating from schooldays in Galloway. It was perhaps not surprising that Macartney became engaged to Borland's daughter, Catherina (more usually called Catherine). She knew that life in Kashgar would be very different from her safe and comfortable existence in London and set about arming herself with more than drawing-room accomplishments, notably cooking.[47] Given the circumstances she was often faced with, she was also to need a strong dose of courage buttressed by an equally robust Presbyterian faith.

Even while he was in England, Macartney received reports of the happenings in Kashgar, as relayed by his Indian clerk, Munshi Ahmed Din. These were alarming. There had been a rebellion of the Muslim Tungans in October 1895 with substantial defections of Chinese troops to the Tungan side, after several Chinese Government defeats in Singhai Province. However, the Chinese brought in massive reinforcements which obliged the Tungans to offer a surrender. The refusal of the Chinese to accept this and the resulting wholesale massacre of the Tungans simply fanned the flames of insurrection among the tribes, bringing the Tungans to the frontier of Kashgaria. By the spring of the following year grain prices had soared, a situation brought about by the requirements of the Chinese troops. The crisis deepened as the Kashgar Taotai was ordered to send all available troops.

With land taxes rising to meet the demands of the rebellion, law and order was in danger of breaking down. Petrovsky himself demanded protection for Russian lives and property, and at the same time claimed he was unable to feed his Cossacks. Macartney's Munshi was attacked by Chinese soldiers and beaten senseless; the soldiers went unpaid and control appeared to be slipping from the grasp of the authorities, who seemed afraid to punish such offences. Word was spreading about a secret society, the Ko-Lau-Hui, who were clearly fomenting revolt in alliance with the Tungans. Unrest was even widespread among the Chinese army, including its highest ranking officers, with the aim of overthrowing the imperial Manchu dynasty. Petrovsky had boasted that the government would at some stage seek Russian protection and indicated that he was prepared to bring in Russian troops.

However, by the time Macartney returned, the rebellion was over, defeated by the sheer number of troops which the Chinese authorities were able to field. But the insurrection had been 'a close run thing' and there was an underlying insecurity and fear. Yet Macartney's own standing was unaffected, and it was a relief to find that with Petrovsky's departure on leave, his replacement was easier to deal with. However, dealing with the weak, characterless Taotai demanded all Macartney's patience, if only to maintain a semblance of British authority. He had to tread warily, but also not overlook any encroachment on his position.

The first issue was to see to it that those who had assaulted his Munshi were appropriately punished. Other similar incidents included one in which Macartney's horse suffered a knife wound from a Chinese soldier. Despite Macartney's best efforts, punishments were not carried out, simply because officials feared the reactions of their own troops. The matter was eventually raised with the British Minister at Peking and with the Secretary of State for India in 1896, such was the government's concern about any apparent weakening of its authority and prestige, which was particularly important in Chinese eyes. Macartney knew he could not let the matter drop and eventually, in October 1897, at his own insistence, he was present at the flogging of the soldier who had wounded his horse.

Meanwhile, on the pretext of plague in India, the replacement Russian Consul Kolokoloff persuaded the Chinese to close off trade between India and Xinjiang, much to Russia's advantage. The return of Petrovsky from leave served only to exacerbate Chinese resentment against the Russian interferences, while the Russians made it clear to Macartney that they had no intention of allowing an official British consular presence anywhere in Xinjiang, at the same time increasing the number of Cossacks at Kashgar from fifty to seventy-five. It was apparently a never-ending jockeying for position. But Macartney suffered the worst humiliation over the question of Indian traders' rights.

The most important function of Britain's representative was to protect the rights of Indian traders in Xinjiang, often in competition with Russian traders, known as Andijans, who had secured very favourable trading terms from the Chinese. For their part, the Chinese authorities, faced with the overbearing attitude of the Russians, were inclined to succumb to Russian pressure and to avoid confrontation at all costs, particularly under the ever-present threat of Russian annexation on their frontiers. The British agent was at a serious disadvantage with little or no support from the Indian government. A particular issue was the question of representation of the Indians to resolve disputes through the Chinese authorities who were disinclined to take them seriously. (Many of the disputes had arisen because the Andijans, with the Russian authorities behind them, frequently avoided honouring debts to the Hindus.) The Russians apparently had no such difficulty.

At one point, the local Chinese magistrate nullified an agreement he had reached with Macartney in one such dispute and fined several of the Indian traders who had presented petitions, threatening them with flogging and other penalties if they ever entertained an Englishman again. Macartney knew that Petrovsky had played his part in all of this and that he was outgunned. The news spread rapidly through the province and by late 1898 all of Macartney's patient work in promoting British prestige over the years was immediately undone. The next Russian plot against the Indian trade was to attempt to ban the lucrative cultivation of Indian hemp, the chief export from Kashgaria to India. In the end, the Taotai, realising its value to his own purse, agreed that the hemp could be exported to India, but not to Russia. Their representative was increasingly successful in strangling the Indian trade while escalating the dominance of Russian influence on the economy of the province. Macartney commented:

> These incidents, small as they are, have been much commented upon by natives as well as Chinese. The timidity and imbecility of the Taotai stand in painful contrast to the arrogance and prestige of the Russian Consul; and the impression is certainly growing, even among the ordinary people, that this country will eventually pass under Russian control.[48]

The British authorities were at last stung into action, and the Indian Viceroy telegraphed Sir Claude Macdonald, the British Minister in Peking. It was agreed to bring the unfriendly attitude of the Amban of Yarkand to the notice of the Chinese government, but the question of Macartney's proposed joint hearing of disputed cases by the Amban and himself was sidestepped, because, in the opinion of the British, it would involve recognition of Chinese jurisdiction over British subjects. Meanwhile the number of complaints from the Indian merchants increased. The local magistrate turned a deaf ear to these unless he was bribed, as he had persuaded the Chinese authorities to give him a monopoly as broker for the hemp trade – another lucrative avenue for corruption and extortion.

Macartney in desperation telegraphed Sir Claude Macdonald in Peking directly, listing five key points for the security of the Indian traders, including importantly the dismissal of the offending magistrate, that British subjects should be free to elect their own representative, and that in future, all civil suits should be settled jointly by Macartney and the Amban. Despite the Taotai's usual avoidance of the issue, he was agreeably surprised that the Amban of Yarkand, when Macartney travelled there for a showdown, offered no resistance. But behind this there was a larger game: the British had leased the port of Wei-Hai-wei, while offering to lend China the enormous sum required to be paid on the Japanese indemnity after their recent defeats of the Chinese. It was not an entirely satisfactory resolution, since the Amban appointed his own nominee to represent the Hindus and heard many cases in a cavalier manner without Macartney present. The latter was no doubt relieved to proceed on leave to England, leaving Kashgar on 13 August 1898.

CHAPTER NINE

Trouble in Kashgaria

Catherine Borland, engaged in trying out her cooking, was totally astonished when Macartney turned up at the family house without warning and announced that they must be married within the week and set off for the challenging return journey to Kashgar before the winter snows. Later, she was to write that at the time of her marriage she was 'the most timid, unenterprising girl in the world. I had hardly been beyond the limits of my own sheltered home, and big family of brothers and sisters, had never had any desire to see the world, and certainly had no qualifications for a pioneer's life, beyond being able to make a cake.'[49]

The marriage took place in the autumn of 1898, when Catherine was barely twenty-one, at Edmonton in Middlesex, and they set off more or less immediately for what was then described as Chinese Turkestan in Central Asia. The journey of six weeks was to take them through Europe, Russia, over the Caspian Sea, via the trans-Caspian Railway to Andijan, by post-cart to Osh, then over the Tian Shan – the formidable 'Celestial Mountains' – on horseback into China and Kashgar itself. Not speaking any Russian, Catherine felt isolated, but not more so than when, at one train stop, her husband got out at the rear to obtain some boiling water on the platform, and to her horror the train started, leaving her without husband, money, or passport. It was an hour before Macartney, blue with cold, was able to rejoin her with the help of the guard who unlocked the compartment. Later, she expressed her nervousness at a crossing of the Oxus over a dilapidated wooden bridge which took half an hour with a guard preceding the train with a red flag examining the beams which had fallen into the swollen river since the last train crossed.

The next stage eastwards beyond Samarkand would have had to be travelled in covered cattle trucks, the floors covered with straw, had it not been for a kindly Russian General who arranged for the Macartneys to travel in a first-class carriage which he had arranged for his daughter's journey in a few days time as far as Margillan. Again their luck was in when they were offered a railway truck, albeit quite unheated, occupied by a single Russian officer who invited them to share it for the journey to Andijan, the terminus of the Central Asian Railway, in company with the famous African explorer John Speke, whom they encountered quite fortuitously. From Andijan to Osh took a whole day in an unsprung *tarantass,* or post cart, drawn by three galloping horses, which gave the travellers an uncomfortable, dust-covered ride.

At Osh, Catherine was pleased to rest for several days in comfortable quarters while the caravan for the mountain crossing – a journey which would take sixteen days – was got ready. After a convivial dinner with the family of the Russian district officer, they purchased from him a small harmonium to accompany a little portable piano being sent out from England – the harmonium necessitating for its transport a continuously grunting yak, with its Kirghiz handlers. This beast was followed by nine baggage horses ahead of the travellers and the two servants from Kashgar who had met them at Andijan. Catherine, quite unused to horse-riding, suffered agonies and cried herself to sleep after the first day's journey, exhausted and bitterly homesick.

In a few days, she was able to marvel at the spectacular mountain scenery. In five days, they came to the foot of the big pass, Terek Dowan, at 13,000 feet, where the yaks trampled a path in the snow for the less sure-footed horses to follow. Catherine gives a very vivid description of the white silence, the sensation of mountain sickness and the goggles worn to protect the eyes against snow blindness. She was quite over-awed by the spectacle from the summit, the path barely wide enough to accommodate the passage of the animals. Here was one of the grandest mountain vistas in Asia with snowy summits and mirror-like glaciers stretching as far as the eye could see. It made a deep impression. After passing over the frontier, the party had the unusual experience, arranged by Macartney, of staying in a Krighiz encampment, described in considerable detail by Catherine who was quite euphoric about her beautiful valley surroundings and their reception by the nomads, surrounded by yaks and camels.

Their entry to Kashgar was akin to a triumphal procession, with a comfortable carriage provided by the Russian consul accompanied by an escort of mounted Cossacks, while along the route, more and more people of every nationality in the district joined the entourage, laying out welcoming food and drink, so that by the time they arrived at Chini Bagh, they were surrounded by hundreds of horsemen, all enveloped in clouds of dust. The house and garden were gaily and elaborately decorated and a Hindu guard of honour in spotless white was drawn up – Catherine, seeing their deep salaams and symbolic offering of rupees, must have felt like a princess. She was delighted to be welcomed by the Swedish missionary Högberg, with his fluent English, even if she felt that her dishevelled and dust-covered travelling condition detracted from a more dignified homecoming.

At Chini Bagh, she found a bachelor house with little provision for creature comforts. The unpainted furniture had been crudely constructed by Macartney and his long-term friend Father Hendriks, and Catherine set about making it more homely and feminine. Later, travelling visitors were to remark on how successful she had been with the minimum of materials. Despite her excellent relations with her kindly servants, she felt obliged to do much cooking herself, being unable to rely on the native cook. She recorded a number of culinary disasters.

Her great joy was the garden, which provided solace especially in the early years, in times of almost overwhelming homesickness, exacerbated by the obstacles of language, especially when Macartney was away from Kashgar. Here, every sort of fruit was grown, including English apples, pears, plums and cherries from cuttings sent out from home to be grafted on to the native stock, while a vinery provided plentiful grapes. For Macartney, Catherine's presence not only ended years of loneliness, but together with their later family, consolidated his position in the Kashgar community, confirming that he had no intention of being a temporary resident. There is no doubt of the love and strong mutual support which they gave to each other in this alien environment.

They certainly were in need of their close and supportive relationship when a series of incidents, several of which had occurred in Macartney's absence, put great pressure on his diplomacy and his sense of duty. Firstly, there had been several assaults on British subjects, including one on the consulate Munshi and on the English Captain Henry Deasy on survey work. However, this was minor compared with the trouble brewing over the allocation of land to the Sarikolis (who were not residents of Kanjut or residents of Hunza) in Raskam by the Amband of Yarkand under pressure from the Russians. Things came to a head early in 1899 when the Russians threatened a military intervention if the order to restore this land to the Hunza inhabitants was implemented, while the Chinese responded by sending reinforcements to the garrison at Kashgar. However, it was clear that the Chinese at every level, from the Peking Government down to the Amband at Yarkand and the totally inept Taotai at Kashgar, were in mortal fear of the power of the Russians, and under pressure would always crumble. Meanwhile, in Kashgar itself, the Chinese officials openly ignored the instructions of the Taotai.

As if all this was not enough, Macartney found that, in his absence, the partnership system that he had previously agreed with the Chinese authorities for the resolution of disputes involving Indian traders was being flouted and that some 600 cases awaited resolution. Macartney decided that, despite the huge workload involved, he himself would take over the settlement of these disputes. However, the Chinese refused to allow the Hindu moneylenders to charge interest and required them to find a third party for surety – a double bind which reduced the Indian trade almost to zero. There was clear evidence that all this had come about by pressure from the Russian traders, the Andijans, supported by Russian officials. The most notable among the latter was of course Nicolai Petrovsky.

What was becoming clearer by the day was that the Russian consul, backed by the Russian War Office, was able to sidestep the views of the more diplomatic Russian Foreign Service, and that the Chinese authorities seemed quite incapable of offering any resistance to their bullying tactics. While Kashgaria was the Russian 'point of the spear' there was a real possibility that they might be able to occupy the whole of Xinjiang if they so wished, initially by economic displacement. What was obvious to Macartney and others was that Petrovsky was quite capable of using all his energies to destabilise both the Chinese and the British through sheer attention to detail and exploitation of any opportunity to create trouble, usually by putting pressure on powerless local Chinese officials. For Macartney, it was a hugely frustrating and demanding time. Given his renowned reticence, it is not known whether he confided in Catherine: although she would undoubtedly have been sympathetic, her youth and inexperience of this strange diplomatic world would have limited her understanding of its nuances.

An example of Petrovsky's pettiness towards anyone friendly with Macartney was his long-standing personal campaign against the now elderly Father Hendriks, who on Macartney's return to Kashgar, was seeking alternative accommodation to avoid intrusion at Chini Bagh. Because of Petrovsky's interventions, this proved extremely difficult, even to the extent of one offer being withdrawn at the latter's insistence. He meted out the same treatment to the Swedish missionaries who had not only become great friends with the Macartneys, but had asked the British agent to be their consul – quite enough for Petrovsky to foment trouble against them: in April 1899, a gang attacked the site of their new mission house and destroyed the building. Despite the various provocations, Macartney refused to rise to the bait of provoking an open clash, which seemed to be the Russian consul's intention in order to break relations: Petrovsky on more than one occasion, palpably discourteous, refused to see Macartney on the flimsiest of pretexts. In the end, the two men did not exchange so much as a single word between November 1899 and June 1902.

In the midst of this, Macartney was learning that wherever the opportunity arose, he had to take a more pro-active approach with the local Taotai, who was both fearful and helpless. When in the first week of 1900 two new officers arrived at the Russian consulate in Kashgar, and when Petrovsky announced to the Taotai that he was sending an officer and five Cossacks to Tashkurgan, Macartney knew that this signalled the establishment of a new Russian outpost in the disputed Sarikol district. Macartney went so far as to draft in Chinese the letters he wished the Taotai to send to the provincial headquarters at Urumchi and his reply to Petrovsky, emphasising to the Chinese authorities the loss in their prestige if the Russians were successful in their thrust towards Sarikol. The Taotai, despite his fears of Russian rejection, was happy enough to sign the letters, while Macartney informed the British Minister in Peking. The provincial governor refused the Russian 'request.' and Petrovsky predictably 'hit the roof,' with a litany of complaints about the lack of Chinese supervision of their frontiers and the illegal traffic in heroin.

As he conveyed it to his superiors, Macartney was quite clear that Petrovsky's intention was:

...to multiply these grievances to show up to his government the shortcomings of the Chinese administration in its worst light, and thereby to urge upon the Cabinet in St Petersburg the absolute necessity of an intervention in order, forsooth, to put an end to a state of affairs in Kashgaria which for Russia is intolerable. Nor is Mr. Petrovsky unassisted in this aim by the Taotai himself whose incapacity to argue a question in a statesmanlike manner is constantly leading him into dangerous concessions.[50]

Macartney continued to try to stiffen the Taotai's resolve, but let it be known to the British Minister that the situation would not be improved until the Taotai was replaced. The matter was taken up by the British Ambassador at St Petersburg, but despite the confirmation of the Russian Foreign Office that the previous agreement over the Raskam allotment still stood, and that Petrovsky had exceeded his authority, this did not seem to restrain the Russian consul, who continued his war of attrition, especially by fabricating underhand dealings by the British. He even insinuated that Macartney was bribing the Taotai – and there was more. What with his negotiations for the establishment in Kashgar of a Russian-Chinese bank with wide economic powers, and proposals to set up Russian factories, Petrovsky was clearly bent on Russian domination of the economy of the province, as a precursor to effective political control.

At a time when Macartney was beginning to wonder if he was 'superfluous to requirements', belated recognition of his efforts to fly the flag in Kashgar came in the form of his appointment as Companion of the Indian Empire, after ten grinding years. Equally satisfactory was his pay increase and change in status as an authorised political officer, with the same conditions of service and leave as his British counterparts. But within a short time, his future prospects were to be threatened by an unexpected turn of events, which swept through China like a bush fire.

The Boxer Rebellion started in Central and North China and was brought about by a combination of factors, among them resentment at Christian proselytising (which was seen by some as simply the vanguard of imperialism and exploitation), and the introduction of opium. The feelings of anger were fuelled by severe drought and flooding in the years between 1898 and 1901, causing thousands of deaths and much destitution, while the ruling Quing dynasty was seen as incompetent and unable to prevent foreign penetration. Even a superficial reading of 18th and 19th century Chinese history indicates clearly how the great powers of the day regarded the country as ripe for exploitation and trading concessions, by force if necessary, as exemplified by the notorious nineteenth century Opium Wars, which the Chinese rightly call "The Century of Humiliation".

In the ensuing chaos, although there were massacres of both European missionaries and Chinese Christians, Xinjiang, like many other provinces, emerged relatively unscathed. This was not the case in Peking, where between 20 June and 14 August 1900, the British legation was under siege and provided sanctuary for almost five hundred foreign civilians, including several hundred foreign diplomats and their families, and several hundred soldiers, besides three thousand Chinese. The siege could be lifted only by the largest international military force ever mounted, comprising some twenty thousand troops.[51] The discords in both the Imperial Chinese army and among the rebels meant that they were easily defeated by the European powers, aided by Japan with their superior organisation, armaments and firepower. The British Minister, Sir Claude Macdonald,[52] who was in charge of the British Legation, remarking on the sterling efforts of the defenders (of whom 17 died and 126 were severely wounded) singled out for praise two young women:

> ...especially commended are two young ladies – Miss Myers and Miss Daisy Brazier – who daily filtered the water for the hospital, in tropical heat, and carried it

with bullets whistling and shells bursting in the trees overhead – a small indication of the conditions during the siege.[53]

Before that, remote Kashgar had been rife with rumours, and by late July 1900, Macartney reported general panic in the district, with the possibility that some Chinese might use the opportunity to take their revenge on the imperious Petrovsky, who had made no secret of his open contempt for the Chinese and their officials. There were reports of Russian troops massing at the border and rumours of an impending attack on the Russian consulate, with Chinese troops making threatening gestures.

Macartney knew he had to act decisively and let the unnerved Taotai know that the Chinese military were more or less inviting a Russian invasion by their foolish actions, with the likelihood of a break-down in law and order. The situation was made even more unsettling by the activities of a group known as the 'gamblers' – disaffected ruffians who preyed on travellers and others on the outskirts of Kashgar.

In his reports, he makes frequent references to these 'gamblers': whereas elsewhere that term might be applied to individuals, gambling was a national addiction in China, often accompanied by drug addiction; those involved often formed themselves into criminal gangs, even preying on the ill-paid and undisciplined army.

Macartney saw a crisis looming as a result of the activities of these gangs, in a situation of general breakdown in law and order, which the Russians could exploit for their own purposes. He set out three essential conditions to stabilise the local community in and around Kashgar, including stopping discussion of the Boxers in the presence of subordinates who might spread more rumours, rescinding the order for the early closing of the city gates, and importantly, keeping up an appearance of friendship with the Russians. For once, the Taotai implemented his advice in full, and a degree of calm prevailed. Eventually, after the siege of Peking was lifted, the rebel leaders were executed. One effect however was to strengthen the position of the Russsian 'hawks' so that in Kashgar, Petrovsky was in a stronger position than ever.

CHAPTER TEN

Archaeologists at Large

In her book on her experiences in Kashgar, Lady Macartney wrote:

As long ago as 1893, my husband acquired a quantity of broken pottery, stone, metal seals, and stucco figurines of Buddha, and some thirty-five leaves of manuscripts – all things he bought in the bazaar from native 'treasure-seekers', evidently picked up by them in the desert. He looked upon his acquisitions as so many curios; nevertheless he sent them to the late Professor Hoernle, once a well-known Sanskrit scholar in Calcutta. What was his surprise when the Professor wrote to tell him that these manuscripts were the oldest hand-written documents then known to exist: they were of the fourth century A.D.[54]

Hoernle's men were enthusiastically dispatching to him their latest purchases as the dealers and treasure hunters kept them supplied. A typical entry from the list of acquisitions in Hoernle's report reads: 'From Mr. G. Macartney, a collection of miscellaneous antiquities procured from Khotan and the Taklamakan, consisting of (a) thirteen books (b) pottery (c) coins (d) sundry objects. Seven books and the antiquities were purchased by Mr. Macartney in Khotan for Rs. 95; the remaining six books were purchased by him from Badrudin [a native dealer]. The total cost was Rs.150. The collection was received by me early in November, 1897.' He singles out Macartney in Kashgar for particular praise among his suppliers, explaining that due to his close proximity to the Silk Road sites, he had proved the most successful in his contributions to the collection.[55] The objects in the large

Hoernle Collection in London were largely put together later by Macartney.

Catherine goes on to relate how Petrovsky, the Russian consul, began to take an interest in this subject, as a result of the ancient manuscript finds of Captain Bower, a British traveller in Kashgaria, and the discoveries in the Lop Nor area by the illustrious Swedish explorer, Sven Hedin in 1900. Oriental scholars throughout Europe woke up to the treasures that the province might contain, and subsequently many scientific expeditions were sent, bent on excavating remote sites around the Taklamakan Desert, including those led by the German Dr A. von Le Coq and the indefatigable Aurel Stein, both of whom became firm friends with Macartney. As a result of his discoveries, Stein was to become one of the most outstanding archaeologists of the 20th century.

The manuscripts themselves were written in a great variety of languages, some of them extinct, on many different materials, from birch-bark to silk cloth, and range in date from the first to the eighth century AD, including portions of Syriac writing of the New Testament, relics from the time of the Nestorian Christian communities in Chinese Turkestan. The subjects included pictorial art in the form of Buddhist wall paintings in caves and stucco reliefs, showing influences from all parts of the Middle and Far East. The sites have proved to be among the most important archaeological sources in the world, right up to the present time, such that there is an ongoing prestigious international scientific project to continue this work.

Macartney's name appears quite frequently in the XII International Congress of Orientalists held in Rome in October 1899, when a number of experts from various countries debated the results of most recent research. An indication of the tenour of the times can be obtained from King Umberto's opening remarks:

> The significant discoveries of a century drawing to a close, have allowed us to get closer to those peoples which, isolated from humankind, had closed their

doors to progress, thus sealing their fate to eternal stagnation. After many efforts, modern civilisation has now won over, forcing them to open their doors and to submit to the inescapable laws of human cooperation, so that everyone can share the triumphs and achievements attained by others. …it is your knowledge of things oriental which is the bright star which reaches the furthest corners of the globe and brings these people out of their centuries-old darkness.[56]

One wonders how this was received by the indigenous delegates from India and China, for example.

Hoernle himself provided a paper on the British Collection of Central Asia Antiquities and presented a translation of Aurel Stein's *Chronicle of the Kings of Kashmir*, while Sergei de Oldenburg spoke on the subject of manuscripts and scrolls provided by Petrovsky. He acknowledged that the largest collection of manuscripts and objects had been provided by Macartney, now to be officially referred to as the 'Macartney MSS.' He also acknowledged that all these antiquities had been obtained from native treasure-seekers and subsequently purchased for what Hoenrle described as 'trifling amounts of money', but because of this, little or nothing was known of their provenance.

The Macartneys received and hosted all of these archaeological explorers and Macartney himself provided advice and, importantly, crucial logistical support for their demanding expeditions. Of these, it was perhaps the most famous of all, Aurel Stein, with whom he established a close rapport and who generously acknowledged Macartney's help, not only before starting out, but during his extended periods in the deserts of Khotan on the edge of the Taklamakan.

While teaching in Lahore in 1898, Stein had developed an interest in researching the ancient sites of Chinese Turkestan, especially the centres of Buddhist culture in

Khotan. To catch the eye of the Indian administration in his proposals of 10 September 1898, he emphasised that these discoveries were undoubtedly of Indian origin and character, while previous finds by native treasure-seekers required verification. Slyly, he mentioned impending Russian expeditions to southern Turkestan and the resumption of Sven Hedin's explorations. Fortunately, Lord Curzon was an archaeological enthusiast and approved, together with Government funding.[57] Stein said:

> I cannot doubt that the sympathetic attitude adopted from the first by the provincial administration to my work was directly due to the efforts made on my behalf by Mr G Macartney CIE[58] the representative of the Indian Government at Kashgar whose personal influence among all Chinese dignitaries of the province is as great as it is well deserved. My narrative shows the manifold benefits I derived from the unfailing care of this kind and accomplished friend, who from afar never ceased to follow my explorations with watchful interest.[59]

The narrative referred to was the acclaimed *Sand-Buried Ruins of Khotan* from which many of the extracts here are taken. Macartney was equally complimentary about Stein, his indefatigability and expertise, which he expressed in his review of Stein's work *Innermost Asia*, specifically on his third expedition.[60] He is, if anything, even more complimentary about Stein's topographic mapping of:

> nothing less than the whole length and breadth of Chinese Turkestan, as comprised between the Tien-shan and the Kun-lun Ranges, and a part of westernmost Inner China as well; in other words, practically all territory enclosed between the 75th and 102nd degrees of longitude and the 35th degrees and 44th degrees of latitude has been mapped anew....in the comfort of our civilised surroundings, how difficult it is for us to realise what these results have

meant in terms of hardships undergone, of dangers incurred, and above all of diplomacy called into action…it is characteristic of his (Stein's) placid and self-reliant nature that he dismisses lightly, with a few words 'threatening Chinese obstruction,' the unfriendly attitude adopted towards him in 1913 by the revolutionary authorities in Hsin-chiang.[61]

On the first of several visits to Kashgar, Stein said:

I found myself welcomed in the heartiest fashion by Mr and Mrs Macartney. Comfortable quarters adjacent to the garden were awaiting me, and when after a needful change I joined my hosts in their dining room, there was every little luxury to favour the illusion that I was in an English home far away from the Heart of Asia ….it was a delightful change to the well-ordered surroundings of my friends' home…there was ample reason to feel grateful for the peace and leisure thus assured to me.[62]

The mounting of such expeditions was a formidable feat of organisation, obtaining supplies, suitable personnel and transport animals, let alone often delicate negotiations with the Chinese authorities *en route* which required no less than five weeks preparation in Kashgar.

…for almost every one of these tasks I stood in need of Mr Macartney's experience and active help. But great as the facilities were which his official position and local knowledge assured to me, I could scarcely have availed myself of them with full advantage, had not his friendly care surrounded me from the first with all personal care and encouragement…

…Mr Macartney, whom long residence and the power of keen observation have made thoroughly conversant with the economic and social conditions of modern Turkestan, was ever ready to allow me to ransack the storehouse of his knowledge for that information without which the ancient accounts of the country cannot be properly understood. Often when matters of Chinese lore were concerned Mr Macartney would summon to our discussion Sun-San-yich, the "Chinese Munshi" of the agency...[63]

Commenting on his visits to the Taotai, and his induction by Macartney on the form and etiquette of Chinese manners, Stein stated:

I could not have wished for more effective help than [that] which Mr Macartney ... [had] already accorded to me.

Already the initial visits which I was able to pay in his company to the Tao-tai, or Provincial Governor and the other chief signatories were under such expert guidance most instructive to me and full of interest. In the course of these visits, followed as they were by "return calls" and other less formal interviews, I was introduced to at least a rudimentary knowledge of the "form" and manners which Chinese etiquette considers essential for polite intercourse. It was no small advantage to receive this instruction through a mentor so familiar with all Chinese notions and ways as Mr Macartney. That the efforts which Mr Macartney undertook on my behalf proved entirely successful was due largely, I believe, to the personal influence and respect he enjoys among all Chinese officials of rank in the Province.[64]

In her biography of Stein, Jeannette Mirsky gave her opinion that:

Stein's friendship with the Macartneys has the air of inevitability about it. Far more than a relationship between two men in the service of the government of India who were thrown together in Chinese Turkestan, it was a meeting of temperament and, deeper than that, an emotional orientation. In both, unassuming exteriors belied a tenacity of purpose tempered by a deep-seated courtesy – qualities which won for Stein the expedition which had brought him to Kashgar and for Macartney, an influence, though long devoid of power, played a vital role in the remote but strategic post where British, Russian, and Chinese interests were responding to political manœuverings.[65]

Such was the opinion of Jeanette Mirsky in her biography of Stein. Although a naturalised British citizen, Stein was Hungarian by birth, and it is speculation that their affinity might have arisen from their awareness of not being wholly British – they had in fact both sailed to India in the same year, albeit with very different prospects. Both men were at heart scholars, and there can be little doubt that Macartney greatly appreciated the opportunity which he had with Stein of engaging in intellectual conversation and the sharing of cultural interests while the archaeologist was at Chini Bagh.

Mirsky goes on to make the following interesting observations:

> The Kashgar post that Macartney held for twenty-eight years symbolised his situation in life. He lived inside China's westernmost boundary in a region different from Nanking, but one that nevertheless could give him the feeling that he had come home; while serving as Britain's representative there, he preserved his filial tie to his father's land. For him Kashgar was the place and the post that validated his parent's marriage... he functioned by virtue of an oft-tested integrity and tact, whose wellspring was his immense sensitivity to deep-seated cultural attitudes – the European contempt for the Chinese and the Chinese contempt for European barbarians.. Accustomed since boyhood to the quicksands of xenophobia, he knew how to keep his equanimity, his equilibrium, and his sanity.[66]

Nor did Stein ignore Catherine's contribution. 'I cannot praise my hostess's hospitality and consideration highly enough,' he wrote to his sister Hetty on 30 Aug 1920. 'How this young woman, married less than a year and a half, manages to run a house in Kashgar that is more English than most of those of Anglo-Indians, is difficult to explain. Trained servants are absolutely unavailable here, and furniture and so forth must be made under the direct supervision of the person ordering it.'[67]

Stein had learned how powerful Macartney's name was with the Hindus established in the oases between Kashgar and Yarkand...business they told Stein, was brisk, 'To protect the interests of this class is a task which the representative of the Indian Government cannot afford to neglect, however unenviable it may be. So I was not surprised that my welcomers were loud in their praises of Mr. Macartney.'[68]

Stein commenced his first journey to the Khotan area in May 1900. Later that year he became suspicious of some of the manuscripts which were offered to him by Islam Akhun in an unknown language, but which he recognised from the Calcutta collections of Prof. Hoernle. Akhun's often highly coloured accounts of his forays into the Taklamakan in search of antiquities had been faithfully taken down from him by Macartney and passed to Hoernle together with the finds – these discoveries found their way between 1895 and 1898 into the great public collections in London, Paris and St Petersburg.

Hoernle examined these over several years, being unable to understand them; other experts did not understand them either. It was Stein who challenged Islam Akhun on their authenticity and in his house uncovered a hoard of similar 'manuscripts' all carefully manufactured by Akhun for his personal monetary gain, which the forger was obliged to admit – with some pride, it should be said. A number of his early and genuine finds had been sold to Balruddin Khan, a rich merchant and the Afghan Aksakal of Khotan, from whom Macartney had made his early purchases in the 1890s. At the XII International Congress in Rome, Hoernle dealt in some detail with his doubts about the authenticity of at least some of these objects, especially the manuscripts, and the unmasking of Islam Akhun, who had deceived Petrovsky, Macartney and several other European scholars with his forged 'old books'.

Stein wrote:

>...when I remembered the great loss of time and labour which the fabrication of Islam Akhun and his associates had caused to scholars of distinction, it was a satisfaction to know that the clever scoundrel had already received from Chinese justice his well-deserved punishment. For fraudulently obtaining from Balruddin...a sum equivalent to about Rs.12 on the strength of a scrawl which he pretended to be Captain Deasy's order, he had been made to wear the wooden collar [the cangue] for a good time, for the imposture practised as Mr. Macartney's agent, he had suffered corporal punishment as well as a term of imprisonment.[69]

Stein is particularly well known for his later discoveries in the Magao Caves ('The Caves of a Thousand Buddhas'), including a copy of the 'Diamond Sutra', the world's oldest printed text bearing any date (AD 868). He removed a large number of objects from the caves, for which he has subsequently been reviled, although at the time this was common practice among European archaeologists. These caves were situated near the oasis of Tunwhang on the south-western edge of the Gobi Desert at an important junction of the Silk Road and the north-south trading route through Tibet and into Mongolia. The amazing discoveries of the contents of these caves are perhaps most lyrically described by the missionaries Mildred Cable and Francesca French in their wanderings in the first half of the 20th century.

By far the most valuable discoveries were made among the manuscripts with block prints. These proved to be a veritable treasure-house of historic data, and among other things showed that in olden times Tunhwang was a centre for learning where men of varying faiths met. There were examples of Uighur script, which is derived from Syriac writing and is known to have been used before the spread of Mohammedism in Central Asia...other manuscripts showed writing in the most ancient known languages...and were more nearly related to the Italic and Slavonic branches of the Indo-European languages than to those spoken in Asia....In addition to this the caves contained many choice specimens of silk, woven in beautiful patterns, which showed to what a high standard the art of silk-weaving had attained long before the time of the Han dynasty.[70]

During this expedition, Stein had the considerable advantage of being kept informed by Macartney of his German and French rivals' movements and progress, whether out of friendship or patriotism is unknown.[71] He returned to Kashgar after his first expedition, which lasted eight months, and with Macartney's help, was able to pack up twelve large boxes of his finds in Khotan.[72] This was modest compared to the collections made during his third expedition, which amounted to 182 cases, most of the contents finding their way to the huge Stein collection housed in the British Museum.[73] Macartney therefore could be said to have been, albeit marginally, complicit in the pilfering of national treasures from China, for which Stein and other collectors have been roundly criticised to this day. Although Macartney did not loot items, but purchased them, the latter would have encouraged looting.[74]

When Stein arrived at Kashgar on 9 June 1906 he was able to report, 'Added to the friendship and comforts of Chini-bagh, was the joyous advent of a new master, the

British Baby Eric, the Macartneys' little son running about the garden'[75] 'Macartney helps me most vigorously to push on with my preparations & thus to keep my start…with Macartney's help I have managed to complete all my preparations.'[76]

Some years later, in 1913, Stein wrote in a private letter, 'Macartney is now the greatest power in the land and able to help in many ways.'[77]

The following narrative by Stein, quoted by Mirsky, gives support for his view:

> … (at Khotan) I was met by a big cavalcade of Indo-Afghan traders with brave old Badruddin Khan at their head and heard that they had just welcomed Macartney outside the West gate. Quite soon I was shaking the hand of my friend and helper to whom I had said goodbye, for years it seemed, only seven weeks ago (this was in late 1913 after an exhausting expedition and – failed – attempt to cross the Taklamakan).[78]

Mirsky reports that, 'the Chinese became increasingly suspicious about his [Stein's] surveying activities and in early 1914 Macartney had to apply to the British Minister in Peking on Stein's behalf for a recommendation to the Chinese authorities to emphasise that Stein's work was purely scientific.'[79]

*

In February 1909, a year after Petrovsky's death, his daughter announced that her father had bequeathed his entire collection to the Museum of the Imperial Russian Archaeological Society, and a year later, Macartney presented to the Russian Academy of Sciences a considerable collection of fragments of manuscripts in Sanskrit and Tocharian.[80]

*

In the contemporary translation and analysis of the International Conference of Orientalists held in Rome in October 1899, Lia Genovese commented on the

The Diplomat of Kashgar   99

remarkable degree of cooperation between archaeologists and scholars from a wide range of nations at that time but added:

> It was only when the potential for rich rewards became clear, that it was necessary to institute official barriers, spheres of influence, outright agreements ... or fictitious partings of the Silk Road into north and south trails to avoid exploration teams or treasure-hunters...

China, the country that would be most affected by these expeditions over the next 25 years, appeared unaware of its own treasures along the Silk Road. Testimony the fact[81] that China's official representative to the Rome Congress delivered a lecture...dealing with contemporary law institutions in China and Japan. The irony is not lost on some readers, who compare China's late arrival with China's strict control of foreign explorations only in 1925-26, after hundreds of crates of priceless artefacts had found their way to museums and art collections around the world...the Silk Road became a romantic notion of the 20th century and a magnet for explorers, scholars, adventurers, botanists, linguists, zoologists, cartographers, engineers, forgers, and armchair travellers. It gave up its priceless treasures to scholars and treasure-seekers, but not without a parting shot, a lasting reminder in the shape of the forgeries, which found their way into venerable institutions in Europe, Asia and America.[82]

Aurel Stein.
The noted Hungarian
archaeologist was a great
admirer of the supportive
George Macartney.
(LHAS)

From L: George Macartney, Colonel Francis
Younghusband, the two British agents Henry Lennard
and Richard Beech after their failed eight-month journey
in 1890
to solve the Turkestan Question. (BLB)

CHAPTER ELEVEN

Russian Rise and Fall

In 1900, Macartney knew that he had to advise the British authorities of the realities of their position in Kashgaria, and in August sent a frank but dispassionate report to the Political Agent at Gilgit. He made it clear that British commercial interests in the area were now minimal and scattered over a wide area, it would be impossible to protect British subjects if further disturbances were to break out. In this event, he would need a guard of twenty infantry to be stationed at Kashgar, requiring the permission of the Chinese government. The British should be prepared, as circumstances dictated, to make Raskam a British zone in order to position troops there against a not unlikely Russian thrust in that area. His proposals fell on deaf ears. Nor was he any more successful in convincing the Taotai of the dangers of withholding legitimate pay (in order to provide for the Peking garrison) from the Chinese soldiers in the district. The situation was exacerbated by the open extortion perpetrated by Lew, the new Amban of Yarkand whose friendly attitude towards Macartney was not to the latter's advantage.

Macartney's second report that year, at the close of 1900, re-iterated the salient points in the first, but also made it clear that he had received no precise instructions for his work in Kashgar,[83] but that he had won concessions from the Chinese in the face of – in his words – 'an indolent and ignorant bureaucracy, which certainly had never given – voluntarily at least – the slightest attention to the interests of our merchants', and only then after incessant badgering. On the second objective of collecting local intelligence, fear of the Russians precluded potential informants from visiting Chini Bagh. Above all, he felt that he had been unable to combat increasing Russian influence, with the Chinese unwilling to put up more active resistance to pressure from that quarter, and with Petrovsky excercising more power than their own rulers, supported by his ministers in Peking.[84]

The economy of the province was now dominated by expanding Russian trade, with thousands of Chinese now dependent on this for their livelihood. In Macartney's opinion, Britain should, under these circumstances, reconsider its entire policy towards Xinjiang, and in particular whether it should continue to strive to maintain the shrinking Indian trade, raising questions about his presence in Kashgar. If his present untenable position there was converted to that of a regular Consul, he believed that the Russians might accept this, if it was made clear that his function was to promote trade and not to seek political objectives; while a reciprocal agreement with the Russians to appoint military attachés in Tashkent and Delhi respectively to exchange news rather than countenance espionage might be acceptable. Unsurprisingly, the British took the line of 'masterly inactivity.' Accepting the likelihood of Russian occupation of the province, while protesting against Russian incursions, with Macartney doing his best to 'hold the fort' was the easier option, even if the strain on their agent would have finished off a lesser man.

On the domestic front, Macartney would at least have been encouraged by the way in which Catherine was coping with a completely alien situation, and despite her inability to communicate with Chinese and other visitors, deriving considerable amusement from what to her were their strange ways – including the almost insurmountable problem, with one Indian lady, of knowing how to indicate, without giving offence, that the visit should end. Several were impressed by the fact that she, as a woman, was able to both read and write, while accompanying herself singing on the piano was a *pièce de resistance*. The piano was only playable as a result of the skills of the Swede, Mr Högberg, who reassembled it after a very rough journey over the mountains.

The little Swedish mission proved a life-saver for Catherine, as the personnel were English-speaking, and she immediately struck up a close rapport with the wives, and with their children. One nine-year old daughter of the Högbergs became especially attached to Catherine, who taught her English. The Swedes no doubt felt equally grateful to the Macartneys for their support in difficult times, as they were sometimes subjected to hostility and even aggression. One of the missionaries, Dr Raquettte, became a distinguished Turki scholar, translating many religious works into Turki.

With the Russian wives, it was a little more difficult, but Catherine was able to socialise agreeably with Mme Kolokoloff and her three children through the medium of French, which typically Catherine set about improving to ease communication. (At one lively Christmas party at the Russian Consulate, apparently some eight different languages were used.) She gives a very colourful pen-picture of Father Hendriks, of whom she was fond, describing him making quantities of wine for the Mass he read every day by himself (apparently having no identifiable converts) using a packing case covered with a dirty lace cloth as an altar, while her husband frequently related how Hendriks had saved *his* own lonely life during his first years in Kashgar.

In her own early days at Chini Bagh, Catherine faced the problem of finding things to do, with servants to look after her needs, and with her husband having constantly to attend to petitioners and other work. She was saved by the departure of her Indian cook, obliging her to resuscitate her culinary skills and at the same time, slowly learning Turki and Hindustani to be able to communicate with the rest of the household who numbered several nationalities, although the Chinese did not approve of her demeaning herself by doing cooking and housework. She gives very amusing descriptions of attempts to obtain milk from the household cow and dealing with meat in a largely Muslim household, including butchering. (Nothing however, prepared her for being obliged – at an elaborate Chinese dinner – to swallow, as an esteemed delicacy, large, gelatinous, black sea-slugs.)

Part of the obligations of the British representative was to provide, at regular intervals, hospitality for the leaders (and their retinues) of the various communities with which he had to deal. Depending on the occasion, this could be made relatively painless by arranging for the appropriate food to be prepared by an outside 'caterer' – in the case of the Chinese, specifying whether this should be a 'first-class' or 'second-class' dinner. On high days, the different communities, whether Indian traders or Chinese officials, would be separated on the terrace by temporary screens and to some extent made their own entertainment with music and informal dancing. Preparing a formal English dinner was quite another matter, involving days of preparation and worrying about sourcing ingredients, not to mention the reception which might be given to such exotic fare as flaming Christmas pudding.

Catherine soon learned to put out only what she intended to be eaten at table, as left-over and transportable items such as biscuits and expensive confectionery might simply disappear into the pockets of departing guests. Catering using other than local ingredients was a problem, as everything had to be transported over long distances, and items from England via India, taking two to three months to come, often arrived in useless condition, including clothing or utensils which had been poorly packed. It grieved the family when mail, carried both by ponies and by mail carriers on foot, was damaged or destroyed, sometimes when the carriers were overwhelmed by avalanches, or swept away by flooded rivers.

Macartney was increasingly aware from 1900 onwards of the rising power and prestige of the Russians, exemplified by their moves into Sarikol, that contested frontier region between Russia and China in the Pamirs, by the arrival of Russian officers there and proposals to build a fort, ostensibly to offset a very modest increase in Indian troops. But that was not the only sign. The Russians insisted on increasing the value of the rouble against Chinese currency (which was actually enforced by a Chinese proclamation under Russian pressure), while local shopkeepers were obliged to accept roubles as currency. The Peking government, faced with the huge war indemnities owed to the Japanese, felt obliged to withdraw their subsidy to Xinjiang and to raise transit dues on all goods passing through the territory, all to the detriment of the British traders, while the Russians were exempt.

While all this was going on, Petrovsky took the opportunity to seek the replacement of any Chinese officials, not wholly supportive of Russian proposals, by other officials who could be pressured into conforming to his wishes, and with the acquiescence of the Peking Government, they seemed not difficult to find. Behind this, there was always the threat of increasing military presence – the ultimate sanction. The Russian bear did not even have to bite – it had merely to growl or bare its teeth. What Petrovsky was aiming for, with the apparent support of Russian ministers, was an increasing degree of control through commercial and economic pressures, backed by subordination of the Chinese administration and political cadres. At this point, in the face of apparent British indifference, Macartney was to report to his superiors 'Russian prestige in Kashgar and Sarikol now carries all before it.'[85]

The issue of Raskam land allocations again raised its ugly head. Petrovsky, asked to consider the allocations which had been made for cultivation and grazing rights, as usual, prevaricated, saying that this required higher approval from Russian authorities. At the same time, it became clear that, by proposing appointments sympathetic to Russian interests, and spreading rumours of British intentions, he was hoping to foment discontent among the Kanjutis – a favourite ploy of the Consul. These were British subjects, although tribute was paid by the Mir to China. (This contradiction was never resolved during the British reign in India.)

Meanwhile, in Kashgar, the recently established Russo-Chinese Bank was offering to help with the crushing Japanese indemnity payments in return for lucrative 'concessions', thus exerting further control on the resources of the country, but including the resumption of internal trading tariffs and customs dues going back some ten years – but not applicable to Russian traders. (While Russian silver was acceptable, it was made clear that Indian silver was not.) A Russian post office was established in Kashgar and it was proposed to extend the telegraph to that city, while establishing a barracks at Tashkurghan for twenty soldiers.

Before he left Kashgar on leave, Macartney decided to try to end the feud between himself and the Russian Consul and called formally on Petrovsky. He was received effusively, as well he might be, Petrovsky appreciating that the Russian star was in the ascendant. Macartney might have been mildly relieved that at least overtly courteous relations might have been resumed. Yet he was quite aware of the 'smile on the face of the tiger.'

The Macartneys did the return journey on leave no less than six times during their time in Kashgar, but for Catherine, the first homecoming was especially exciting, even if it had to be delayed to avoid clashing with the Munshi's own leave to see his family in India. Neither she nor her husband appreciated being under almost close guard while crossing Russian Turkestan, escorted by Cossacks who watched their every movement, at a time when the British were under particular suspicion. However, their travails nearly ended when one of the horses pulling their coach took fright crossing a river bridge and the coach slewed violently, breaking both the shaft and the edge of the bridge, leaving the coach hanging precariously over the torrent. Macartney had to intervene to prevent the Russian officer in a demonic frenzy beating the driver to a pulp. Although they were unhurt, the Macartneys were badly shaken as was the horse which shied at everything on the road to Andijan. Even on the train journey westwards, a guard was posted outside their compartment, following them to the dining car and accompanying them on walks at stops: it was an intimidating experience.

By the time they set off in February 1904, over a year later, on their return to Kashgar, a second child, Eric, had been born and had to undertake the perilous journey at the age of five months. A nurse – a devoted family retainer in Catherine's parents' household – was recruited. The young child stood the journey better than anyone else, fed on patent baby food mixed with cold boiled water and sleeping in the body of his perambulator. Arriving in Kashgar on 8 April 1904, the Macartneys found that Petrovsky had returned to St Petersburg the previous year on leave, apparently not in the best of health: he was not to return. In the meantime, the British Government had been pressing, albeit somewhat late in the day, for the establishment of a full Consul post at Kashgar, for once supported by the British minister in Peking, Sir Ernest Satow.

When the Macartneys returned to Kashgar in the spring of 1904, the political situation had changed significantly in respect of the balance of power in Asia. In January 1902, Britain had signed a formal treaty of alliance with Japan, securing Japanese recognition of British interests in China, thus diminishing Russian influence there, while recognising Japanese interests in Korea. The Russians however were not amused, but found themselves blockaded by the Japanese at their crucial access to the Eastern seas at Port Arthur. The following naval battles between Japan and Russia proved disastrous for the latter and Russian prestige in Asia plummeted. By early 1904, reports of the Russian defeats were reaching Kashgar, but equally significantly, it was impinging on the Chinese population that, for the first time, a European power had been overwhelmed by an Asian one. It encouraged incipient Chinese revolutionary thought and action against what they rightly considered barbarian invasion and oppression.

Macartney was now officially the British Consul in Kashgar, although this was not recognised by the Chinese Government, but the situation with the Russians had not materially changed, with the important exception that they were said to be massing substantial numbers of troops to the borderlands at the same time as the Russians were still at war with Japan. and that the army of Turkestan was being fully mobilised. The good news was that Petrovsky, having retired from public service, was replaced at the Kashgar consulate by his former secretary Kolokoloff, with whom Macartney could at least have friendly relations, and even appeared to espouse the revolutionary cause. (Kolokoloff went so far as to confide to Macartney that he had received instructions not to recognise Macartney as consul.) Relations with the Chinese however continued to be compromised by lack of cooperation, particularly over the question of trader nationality and prohibitive customs dues. Meantime the British government made it clear that Macartney was not to assume the title of Consul until current negotiations over Tibet were completed.

In 1905 proposed road improvements to Kashgar from Naryn became a three-cornered issue, with the Russians pressing for upgrading to accommodate wheeled traffic, while Macartney alerted the Taotai to its possible military implications as a potential invasion route. Initially the Taotai stood firm, but gave way eventually when a contract was signed with the Russo-Chinese bank allowing it a monopoly of all transport of goods, mail and passengers between the Russian railhead at Andijan and Kashgar, in return for an annual payment for improvement and upkeep of the road. It was a strategic triumph for the Russians.

Macartney had his suspicions about the involvement of the notoriously venal Taotai, who enjoyed an unusually luxurious lifestyle.

However, all was not going well for the Russians. In the same year, there were bloody riots in St Petersburg, the peasants revolted against the aristocracy and estate owners, and a general strike in October paralysed the country. Only the promise of an elected *duma* temporarily quietened the unrest, giving enough breathing space for the Tsar and Russian government to re-assert their authority, often brutally. But Macartney had other troubles to sort out. At Yarkand, there was serious conflict between the Muslim community and the mainly British-Hindu traders. Much of this stemmed from the activities of the Shikarpuri money-lenders who were pressing for debts to be settled, mainly incurred by gamblers: Macartney had little time for them, but had to be seen to be even-handed. He let the Indian government know that the flood of money-lenders coming into Kashgaria was not reflecting well on the British. In March 1907, an incident in Yarkand threatened to spill over into real inter-religious strife. The Chinese Amband, hearing that Macartney was on his way, stood to one side.

He was met by an angry mob of five to six thousand people, headed by the Andijans, who jostled him, shouting accusations at the Hindus. Macartney spoke forcibly to the crowd in Persian, ordering some of the least tractable Hindus to be beaten and the rest to give a sum of money to the mosque and to salaam before it – the Hindus had been accused of being disrespectful towards the mosque. In return, the Yarkand Muslims were not to kill cows or sell beef near the Hindu quarters. Macartney was particularly relieved that acceptance of his edict meant that not only were lives saved, but any attempt by the Russians to exploit the situation, especially through the Andijans, was foiled. His erstwhile colleague Younghusband let the Indian Government know that Macartney's action, by a combination of tact and ability, had pre-empted a very dangerous situation. Further, Younghusband recommended that Macartney should be given an escort of Indian troops for his protection, to which the Government's bureaucratic response was that this could follow only from a regular consular appointment.

Changes on a wider front were afoot when Russia signed a convention with Japan, respecting their territorial claims to Manchuria and Korea respectively, and importantly, guaranteeing the integrity of China. Soon afterwards this was followed by a convention which respected British interests in Afghanistan and Persia, with Tibet as a neutral buffer state, part of the subsequent Triple Entente between France, Britain and Russia. Although this made for easier relations with the Russian Consulate in Kashgar, Kolokoloff was gloomy and pessimistic about his own country's future, with its financial troubles and lack of effective democratic government. At the same time, the local Chinese population was becoming less tolerant of foreigners and inclined to haughtiness, more especially in the matter of settling traders' cases, and there was also a growing agitation among the populace for reform.

CHAPTER TWELVE

His Britannic Majesty's Consul-General

On 30 June 1908, Macartney and his family left Kashgar on leave. Two months later, his temporary replacement, Captain Shuttleworth, was told by telegram from Peking that the Taotai had been instructed to recognise him as His Britannic Majesty's Consul in Kashgar. After eighteen years of laborious work there, it is ironic that this notification should come when Macartney was out of the country. It was also very obvious that the Chinese attitude, now not overshadowed by the threatening power of its overbearing neighbour, had allowed this recognition as a direct result of the Anglo-Russian Convention. It was nevertheless a personal triumph for Macartney who had hung on through thick and thin, conscientiously and with the greatest integrity, doing what he undemonstratively saw as his duty with minimal recognition.

For the journey home, the family decided to return by a novel route via Naryn and Chimkent, each on one of the branches of the old Silk Road (in what is now Kyrgystan), to avoid several difficult crossings of flooded rivers on the usual route via Osh. At Aris, they were to join the Orenburg railway just to the north of Tashkent. With two and a half year-old Eric and five year old Sylvia, accompanied by their nurse and two servants, it was to be a considerable undertaking, involving much preparation. After three days of driving over the hot plains in little Russian carriages, the party mounted ponies with the children seated on long saddles in front of the servants, arriving at their first Kirghiz camping ground after a tiring ride of twenty-seven miles. Next day they faced the difficult Karatecki Pass where Catherine related how 'there seemed to be no road at all over the great black jagged rocks.'

The loaded pack ponies had to be led carefully down through the boulders, and the children were put into home-made travelling sacks carried on the backs of the servants, with all the mounts tied together, bridle to tail. Their nail-biting descent was rewarded by a flowery meadow for a campsite and a local Kirghiz reception party. The next day saw them on the heights of the Tian-Shan mountains, having crossed and re-crossed the Chakmak River many times. Despite being mid-summer, a bitterly cold wind swept over the plain, and they all felt the effect of altitude sickness. On the following day, they crossed the Chinese-Russian border at the Turgat Pass and the watershed of the Tian-Shan. They were delighted by the ride down the other side through undulating flower-filled meadows, with their populations of scampering marmots, which the children imitated, and were hospitably welcomed by their Kirghiz hosts.

After a long, hot, and fly-ridden ride, they left their horses at At-Bashi, but not before a frightening crossing of the river of that name, with the horses almost out of their depth. Here again, they were almost overwhelmed by the hospitality of their local hosts, sleeping in proper beds for the first time since leaving Chini-Bagh. Catherine described her nervousness at being driven the next day in a *tarantass* over the horrendously steep passes with perpendicular drops on both sides, where the driver had no option but to allow the three horses their head. The contrast to their previous experience with suspicious Russian 'guards' could not have been greater when they reached Naryn, where the Russian District Officer was pleased to show them the sights of the bustling township and where they spent several days awaiting transport. The next stage was enlivened by the collapse of one of the carriage wheels which necessitated the nurse, Fanny, and Eric all being crammed in the remaining carriage to limp into the post station at Kara-unkur – a primitive log cabin at the foot of the forest. Here Catherine, with the aid of *Elliman's Embrocation* and some massage, scored a success by reviving an aged villager who appeared initially to be on the point of death.

On the second day out from Kara-unkur, another collapsed wheel had to be replaced, thus losing precious time. That was a minor inconvenience compared with the flies and penetrating dust they encountered on several days crossing the steppes, and procuring food proved a problem. One of the days was simply a chapter of accidents when, soon after starting, their uncontrollable horses bolted, only stopping when the carriage driver drove up a steep bank at the side of the road. But again the horses bolted while passing some carts and the party was only saved by one of the wheels flying off while they were careering at break-neck speed, stopped eventually by the axle dragging in the dust below the lop-sided carriage.

Even more seriously, at Aulie-ata, Eric had the signs of fever. Several days of jolting and dust did not improve matters, and both the children became unwell, unable to keep food down, while Catherine herself also succumbed. As if this was not enough, coming down a steep hill, the driver lost control of the horses drawing the luggage cart, which then just missed by a hair's breadth the *tarantass* carrying Eric and the nurse. At the bottom of the hill, just before a narrow bridge, the horses were brought to a standstill by three wheels flying off. The incident was a shock to every one. After a very bad night, the party got up at dawn to hasten into Chimkent, where fortunately they found a doctor. He was quite emphatic that they should not proceed for at least a few days and found them quiet comfortable rooms.

They were not to know that the few days were to lengthen into an anxious month, with the children developing dysentery which spread to the nurse. There was even the real possibility that Eric would lose his life. His parents snatched only an occasional few minutes sleep – either on a sofa or the floor in two small rooms shared by the whole party – in between caring for the toddler. At last they resumed their journey towards the railway, but found themselves, after a harness breakage, travelling in the dark on a badly rutted track out in the steppes. Without illumination and with Eric running a high temperature, the last twenty miles took over six hours. They reached Aris late at night to find their quarters shut up, although their kindly Russian hosts made the now completely exhausted travellers as comfortable as possible.

By morning, Eric again had a high fever, but at least they were in the very comfortable house of the Chief Engineer of the Moscow-Tashkent Railway, and by the following day, although Eric was still too weak to stand unsupported, the family felt fit to join the afternoon train, having travelled some eight hundred miles from Kashgar. They journeyed via Moscow, Warsaw and Berlin, spending four very pleasant days with their old archaeological friend, Dr von Le Coq, before going on to Calais and London, arriving there on 7 September 1908. Catherine records that three months after leaving Kashgar, the children were still showing signs of their illness. No mention is made of how the quite elderly nurse, Fanny, coped with this horrendous journey.

Even before the Macartneys left Kashgar, there had been signs of change in China. Recognising their own weakness, China attempted reform of the military, with foreign language education and training in drill. There were also efforts to encourage indigenous exploitation of economic resources, especially coal, petrol, iron and gold and to restrain foreign activities in these fields. None of these was successful, partly because neither the Chinese nor the Turki population had the necessary education and skills of management and administration. At the same time, having seen the example of the development and military success of the Japanese, based on western ideas, the Chinese seemed anxious to copy these, including political reform.

While the Quing dynasty continued to hold a firm grip on power through the Dowager Empress and the continuing appointment of Manchus to all the higher official posts, there were some attempts to establish political institutions. For example, Provincial Assemblies were instructed to meet in 1908, and local district councils, with the power to raise taxes, were required to be formed in the same year. There was increasing pressure from the Turki population to have more say in Xinjiang government, but there was also resentment that these councils were to be presided over by the Chinese.

More particularly, that same population resented the new laws that removed the collection of customs dues from the traders to local officials. Both the Chinese and the Turkis were angered by the restrictions on opium growing and there were not infrequent mass petitions of the Turkis in Kashgar against raised taxes and customs dues. Against this background of discontent, it is not surprising that the Turkis refused to have anything to do with local representation on the proposed district councils, which equally unsurprisingly the Taotai himself resisted. The "gardening soldiers"[86] remained in post, despite the proposal to replace them with disciplined foreign-trained troops. However, corruption and venality at official levels were still rife and attempts to replace the Taotai came to nothing when he apparently succeeded in bribing the Provincial Governor to retain him. According to Macartney, this simply encouraged the nefarious activities of various criminal elements who infested the backstreets of Kashgar. Meanwhile the Taotai had been obliged to borrow large amounts to offset deficiencies in the Treasury.

Against this background, the Chinese began to flex their muscles in attempting to constrain foreign trade privileges, notably those exercised by the Russians, and to prohibit further land acquisitions by foreigners. None of this materially stimulated Chinese economic or entrepreneurial development. However, the attitude of both the Russians and the Chinese towards Britain had changed significantly: 1907 was the turning point when Sir Arthur Nicholson (afterwards Lord Carnock), then British Ambassador in St Petersburg, made a treaty with the Russian Government to bring about a *rapprochement* between Britain and Russia so that they ceased to be hostile. British trade from India now flourished, with Indian imports into Kashgar doubling.

The formal recognition of the British Consul by Russia not only improved relations between these two countries, but also greatly enhanced British prestige with the Chinese, who much approved of the proposal to establish a new British Consulate at Kashgar, especially when it was proposed that the much sought-after medical services and medicines would be offered to Chinese officials as well as to British subjects. (The consulate compound, amounting to a small village, might house between seventy and eighty people, if wives and children are included.)

The Chinese even went so far as to help to settle the debts owed to the Shikarpuris: with a ban on money-lending to Chinese subjects, many of the money-lenders returned to India. It was all a far cry from the days of the predominance of Petrovsky, who having retired to Tashkent, died while Macartney was on leave in England. In the previous year, his successor Kolokoloff was recalled to Russia, where he assisted in revising the Treaty of St Petersburg, including, no doubt to his chagrin, the delaying of import duties on Chinese goods entering Russia. With the death of the Manchu Empress Dowager in November 1908, after forty years rule, the scene was set for yet more dramatic changes in the Chinese scene.

A month after Macartney's return to Kashgar on 1 November 1909, a new Russian Consul, M. Sokov arrived. He did not particularly impress Macartney: Sokov appeared to take little interest in external affairs beyond keeping his office 'ticking over.' However, in mid 1911, a new Secretary, Edward Behrens, was appointed. He was much more bullish in his approach, even going so far as to suggest that Xinjiang was logically Russian territory. He spent considerable energy in compiling a register of Russian citizens in the province and encouraging others to register this as their nationality: the inducement was that Russians had significant trading privileges which made this attractive. His contempt for the Chinese authorities rivalled that of Petrovsky.

The Chinese authorities were now actively attempting to push the indolent Kashgarians into more modern ways, but the establishment of compulsory schooling for both Muslims and Chinese caused considerable resentment, both on religious grounds and because of the resultant increase in taxes to fund these. Macartney was able eventually to convince the Provincial Government that this initiative was counter-productive. The school-building projects were attracting the greedy eyes of the Military Commander as a lucrative source of private finance. At the same time, visitors noted that there was no police force, sanitation or any other public works. There was trouble too with the opium growers being obliged to dig up their crops, resulting in serious riots and the summary beheading of twelve of the ringleaders.

More seriously, a mutiny at the Provincial Barracks at Urumchi provoked riots which destroyed a hundred properties by fire and involved another bout of beheadings of those claimed to be responsible. (All of this Macartney had anticipated, together with the threat to Chinese rule in the Province as a result.) Meanwhile, the Russians and the Chinese were at logger-heads over the trade taxes which discriminated against Chinese goods, while the Chinese were agitating for a revision of the Treaty of St Petersburg. Sokov was dismissive of the Chinese complaints about the ban on marriage between Russians and Chinese. In time, this would inflate the number of those claiming Russian citizenship.

Macartney, dismayed by the continuing irresolution over Hunza and the saga of the Raskam allotments, wrote a long memorandum to the Indian Government proposing a whole slew of proposals for finally resolving these long-running problems, including one which would have given the Chinese consular rights in cities in India in exchange for similar rights for the British in China. Predictably, months later, in February 1911, the Indian government made it clear that no action was necessary on any of this. In the same month, the Russians issued an ultimatum over the revision of the Treaty of St Petersburg, backing up their demands by the massing of troops on the Mongolian border, while in the following month, some thirty-five Cossacks on horseback scattered the market folk in Kashgar, with displays of power elsewhere.

In the middle of all this, Macartney received the King's Commission, appointing him Consul-General at Kashgar. While this undoubtedly helped in further ameliorating the Chinese attitude towards the British – the Taotai was especially helpful over the purchase of land for the new proposed consulate – they bent to Russian pressure over the St Petersburg Treaty. But elsewhere in China, serious trouble was brewing, the touch-paper being the insurrection of Chinese troops in the garrisons of Yangtse and Shensi.

Mrs (later Lady) Macartney in the Chini Bagh garden c.1901, shortly after her arrival at Kashgar. (LHAS)

CHAPTER THIRTEEN

Revolution

In late 1911, in south and central China, city after city joined the rebellion against the Manchu dynasty, demanding political reform under the revolutionary government of Sun-Yat-sen in Nanking. In Xinjiang, the Republican banner was raised at the Provincial Headquarters in Urumchi following the killing of the Tartar military commander, although the city itself successfully held out against the rebels: Macartney was advised by the Chinese authorities not to recognise the latter. Nevertheless he requested an escort of thirty Gilgit Scouts under a British officer, more to deter Sokov (who had requested seventy more Cossacks) from using the turmoil as an excuse to invade. (The British administration cited logistical difficulties as an excuse to refuse this request.) In fact, the revolution barely affected western Xinjiang, mainly because of the confusion of loyalties, with the government troops supporting the old régime. Officials there did not know which way to jump.

In April, events took a more serious turn with the murder of the old Taotai at Aksu together with senior officials. A mob gathered at the yamen in the city and the Republican flag was hoisted. Panic afflicted the authorities in Kashgar, with rapid cutting off of queues (pigtails or braids), the symbol of the hated Manchu dynasty. Macartney's concern was with the so-called 'gamblers' and criminal fraternity who were associating with disaffected soldiers and he reported that he 'feared a scramble for power among the vagabond Chinese'.[87] On 7 May he was summoned to the Russian consulate to be told by Sokov that the Taotai's *yamen* was being attacked by a mob. He returned home to alert his family which now, apart from his wife Catherine, consisted of his elder son of eight and a half years, daughter Sylvia at five and a half, and six-month old Robin. At the time, Macartney's brother Donald was visiting, together with a Scottish minister from Urumchi, Rev. George Hunter.[88] Leaving the house again, Macartney, supported by his Cossack guard, immediately prepared for an attack. (Catherine records that, before he left home, he tried to stuff a revolver in his pocket without her seeing it.)[89]   Catherine notes that, for some peculiar reason, her one thought was that she and the children should be in clean clothes if they were to be murdered and, 'to the surprise of the Russians [who had returned with her husband], 'we all appeared at 4.40 a.m. as though we were going to a garden party, in spotless white!'[90] Meanwhile all the Union Jack flags which could be found were put up round the house and instructions were given to British subjects to do likewise, resulting in many curious hastily home-made flags being posted, while the missionary, Mr Hunter, was ordered to cut off his pigtail (which he had adopted to make himself less conspicuous among the Chinese community) and dress as a European, turning him, in Catherine's words, into 'what he really was, a splendid Scotchman.'[91]

Macartney visited the Tao-tai, who had been in hiding, to find him quite relaxed as he and other Ambans had given large amounts of money to the revolutionary party and thought they had bought them off. Macartney was not convinced.

Later a message was received that the Taotai and the City Magistrate had been assassinated, but the report from the Military Commander was to the effect that foreign nationals were unlikely to be attacked, while recommending that they stay indoors. For much of the day, the Macartneys were engaged in receiving terrified refugee officials and their families hidden in Turki carts. They had had to pass along roads swarming with revolutionaries flourishing blood-stained three-edged swords. Several of the refugees were obliged to stay in tents in the consulate garden for several weeks. One of the first refugees was a totally distraught woman, who had seen her husband hacked to death in bed in front of her. She only succeeded in preventing the murder of her small son by throwing herself on the mercy of the rebels.[92] Both the seventy-two year old Taotai and his wife had been hacked to pieces because, according to the gang, he had been corrupt. Macartney had been right – the tearing down of the Republican flag by the mob indicated that this was the work of disbanded soldiers and criminal associates, who, newly armed, were a genuinely menacing force.

Next day he received news that the New City was in revolt, with Chinese officials killed and shops looted. Later a message from the Russian Consulate stated that loyal troops from the New City were marching on Kashgar to deal with the rebels, and that there *was* a threat to foreigners. There was renewed panic and the Russian quarter was posted with Cossacks. Meanwhile the Chini Bagh community took what precautions they could against surprise. Catherine details their preparations:

> Rolls of bandages were prepared and I packed up the children's clothes and the baby's food into bags in case we found it necessary to run and hide in a place we had already decided on...My husband and his brother even arranged between them how we women and children were to be dispatched if the mob were too strong for us, though I did not know this until long afterwards...our servants armed themselves with any kind of weapon they could find...knives, sticks, old swords, etc...and even our governess, Miss Cresswell, took the big carving knife and steel to bed with her...Having made all preparations possible, we lay down fully dressed, while Donald and Mr Hunter took it in turns to do sentry duty round the house and garden.[93]

When three cannon shots boomed out from the walled town, shaking the house, the Macartneys leapt from their beds to prepare for an attack. But nothing happened: the shots were the salute to the deceased Taotai. It turned out that the rebel march on Kashgar was a fiction, although a mob of mutineers and disbanded soldiers in the New City had run amok and killed a colonel and a high civil official. But a so-called New Regiment had been formed, with about 400 recruits from the various factions, on the promise that they would not be punished for the murders of previous days.

Things had quietened down sufficiently for Macartney and his brother Donald to ride daily through the city without escort, to show their trust that no harm would come to them.[94] Reluctantly, Catherine even let the eight-year old Eric ride with them on his pony to show that they were not afraid: he was mobbed, but by admiring townsmen offering sweets and cakes. Apparently one of them offered a bag of sweets in one hand while he held in the other the still-bleeding head of a victim. Subsequently, unarmed, they rode through the soldiers' camp regularly without being molested. There could hardly have been a better example of the British Empire's 'stiff upper lip'.

There was however a question mark over the actions of the rioting mobs, who seemed no more sympathetic to the newly-established Republic than its predecessors, while the refugees sheltering in the consulates were still in terror of their lives, and Macartney knew there was danger about. In time, it became clear that the malcontents and the disbanded soldiers were out for revenge on the authorities, and above all, for whatever money and goods they could lay their hands on. In all this, it appears that none of the Russian or British-Indian communities were interfered with, which was a great relief to Macartney, so that it seemed that the conflict was entirely within the Chinese population.

What was worrying to him however was that the lack of action against the foreigners was entirely due to fear of the Russians and possible intervention from that source; if they considered that the uprising justified this, they could command the strategic Pamir plateau and the routes to India through Ladakh and Hunza. His concerns were increased when he heard of Behrens's attempts to create incidents in the southern oases which would have been taken as an excuse to justify Russian intervention.

What Macartney feared most came to pass when 750 well-armed Cossacks arrived at the beginning of June, summoned – according to Sokov – to protect both Russian and British interests, despite Macartney's protests that the mutineers had done no violence to anyone but their own countrymen. However, the commanders of the Russian expedition were not amused by the absence of the opposition they had expected. The Chinese approach of offering no resistance and instead offering tea and cakes to the invaders left the army personnel non-plussed and not a little irritated, while the mutineers either kept themselves well out of sight or were ostentatiously cooperative with the newly-appointed Chinese officials.

It was the quick thinking of Macartney however that, in the autumn of 1912, prevented a potential confrontation between the Chinese and Russian forces. The Chinese authorities had decided to transfer some of the revolutionary forces – the Russians were well aware of this – and they marched out of the city late at night.

Macartney, quite by chance, passing the Russian Consulate, saw a whole regiment of Cossacks preparing to march, apparently on the same road that the Chinese soldiers were likely to follow. (This was, according to Sokov, simply to conduct some night manoeuvres.) The likelihood of an 'accidental' encounter in the dark was obvious. Macartney immediately sent a message to the Chinese commander alerting him of this danger and the plans were promptly changed, apparently to the disgust of the Cossacks, spoiling for a fight.

It was not until many months later that Macartney discovered the real forces behind the uprising, namely the activities of the secret society, the Ko-Lao-Hui, who were responsible for much violence and bloodshed in the north-west province of Shensi in particular, with the massacre of hundreds of Manchus and several missionaries, while the society took over the administration of the province. Their methods were particularly vicious, with blackmail, terrorism, kidnapping, robbery and torture being used. It was only Russian intervention and Macartney's steadying hand which prevented this movement from creating the same level of mayhem westwards into Xinjiang in 1912 and 1913. Two tough members of the Ko-Lao-Hui – Hsiung Kao-sheng and an assistant – were dispatched to the province to organise resistance to the Russian intervention.

In mid June 1912, there occurred a series of disturbances at Chira, some 350 miles east of Kashgar. These were sufficiently serious to be reported in the international press. It all started with a local dispute between one Syed Haji, a Muslim Andijan who had taken Russian nationality, and a Turki neighbour over irrigation rights. As so often at this time in Xinjiang, the contestants drew wider support from their communities, in this case fuelled by Behren's machinations in attempting to register as many inhabitants of the province as Russians, while encouraging the Andijan traders to defy the local Amban's decision on the matter, which came down in favour of the Turki. The result was a riot between the Russian Muslims and the Turkis loyal to the government under the very able but ruthless Governor, Yang Tseng-hsin, who was not above liquidating anyone seriously threatening his position.

The Ko-Lao-Hin officials sent into the Province were determined to assert Chinese authority, by force if necessary, at a time when the Russians were making their presence felt in Kashgar. When a force was sent to arrest Syed Haji, several soldiers were killed, while the house where he had taken refuge was set on fire, killing over thirty of his supporters. It was the most serious incident between Russian subjects and the 'gamblers', and one which Macartney had long anticipated in some form. It was a perfect excuse for Sokov to threaten to send two hundred Cossacks to Chira, before Macartney succeeded in calming him down. Unfortunately lurid accounts of the incident appeared in the Russian press, with demands for appropriate punishment directed especially at Hsiung Kao-sheng, who had undoubtedly fomented at least some of the trouble, on behalf of the secret society's nationalistic ideology.

The incident was even reported in *The Times* of London, obliging Macartney to give as accurate account as he could from a distance of several hundred miles from the action. For their part the Russians assured Britain that they had no intention of invading the Province, while the British, anxious to keep Russia on side over the then current issue of Tibetan security, looked the other way: Xinjiang by comparison was unimportant. However, the Ko-Lao-Hui were determined to undermine Russian authority and were successful in exploiting the differences between the Russian army officers and their consulate at Kashgar, where Sokov and Behrens were also at loggerheads over the latter's punitive activities in the southern oases, while the army were disenchanted with the lack of action. Behrens was recalled to St Petersburg to explain himself.

It says something for Macartney's standing and his willingness to provide a listening ear that all of these factions confided in him privately, including a very senior Russian General sent specifically to investigate the Xinjiang problem. It all reflected a conflict at national level between the Foreign Ministry which sought solutions through diplomacy and the Tsarist military machine, supported by its officers. At the end of the day, Governor Yang, under pressure to get a favourable revision of the Treaty of St Petersburg, made a public apology on behalf of the Chinese authorities over the Chira revolt, while sending the Kashgar regiment to Urumchi, thus neutralising the troublesome gamblers. All this was at a time when there was a serious suspicion that the Russians hoped to create a compliant 'independent' buffer state over Xinjiang under the 'kingship' of Mustafa Khan, the grandson of the rebel Ya'qub Beg, by inciting a Muslim uprising. Macartney's reports on these clandestine activities in the autumn of 1912 caused some perturbation in the corridors of Whitehall.

CHAPTER FOURTEEN

Welcome to a New Consulate

In 1913, the new British Consulate-General, based on Chini Bagh, was at last completed. It had taken several years work, since everything had to be started from scratch, even to the selection of growing trees for felling and seasoning over several summers and the building up of a supply of bricks. The first buildings to be erected were the houses for the Munshis and the Hospital Assistant. While the original office buildings were demolished to make way for the purpose-built offices in what was the old house, the cliff overlooking the river and the road was built up and strengthened. The Consulate itself now had an upper storey commanding a very fine view over the surrounding countryside, with the magnificent Pamir Mountains forming the backdrop. Large reception rooms were now separated from the domestic quarters, and central heating from a furnace was installed.

The whole had been planned and designed by Mr Högberg, who brought the Swedish community to help with the papering of all the rooms. Catherine was delighted to have a big, new, airy kitchen with a stove to replace the old iron box fired with charcoal. The now dignified office buildings surrounded a large court-room, in which an imposing portrait of King Edward was hung, while over the main gateway there now stood a regal Coat of Arms sent out by the Foreign Office. The servants had a little mosque and a pond within their own village, each of the houses having its own courtyard. It was all a far cry from the primitive Chini Bagh of old, for which Catherine still had a certain nostalgia.

Social life had developed too within the foreign community, particularly with the enlargement of the

Russian colony and the increase in the military force, and Catherine was able to communicate with the women who spoke French, but generally their habits were too different to make for easy relations. The Russian women rose late, while the British typically had completed their walking or horse-riding well before they did so. (Diana Shipton, while at Kashgar in the 1940s, would take an hour's walk every morning, and in spring and summer, she and her husband Eric played tennis three times a week.) By late afternoon the Russian womenfolk, who rarely took exercise, were elaborately dressed and coiffured, amused that Catherine was up and appropriately dressed for her household duties by seven in the morning. Ella Sykes, who arrived with her brother just before the Macartneys left in 1915 on what was to become their last home leave, noted that Russian women did not get up till midday and that their lunch parties went on until evening. 'Society' lived in one another's houses all day – whereas she and her brother were usually in the saddle by 7.30.

Ella sometimes found the habits of the servants at Chini Bagh difficult:

> When we were seated at table my anxieties were by no means over, for, in spite of my coaching, the waiters were fond of getting into one another's way, and occasionally there were unseemly wrangles between Sattur, who considered he was the head, and masterful Jafar Bai, who would sometimes wrench the bottle of wine from him as he was endeavouring to fill up the glasses of our guests.

She was to say of Sattur that it was a proud moment for both herself and Sattur, when, 'after many a reprimand, he knocked at my bedroom door instead of bursting in without notice.'[95]

The sociable Russians held dinner parties most evenings, and, while everyone was jovial and friendly, the Macartneys often found these a trial, with the excessive drinking and speech-making lasting well into the following morning, while the language barrier seemed to make such occasions interminable. Catherine describes one acutely embarrassing occasion when champagne flowed like water and her two male neighbours at table, in her words 'became more and more confidential with me, till at last I was almost supporting them as they leant up against me.' The Royal Toasts ended with one of her companions, attempting to make an incomprehensible speech, allowing his glass of champagne to be poured down Catherine's dress, apparently the fate of most of her frocks. Her Presbyterian sensibilities would undoubtedly have been offended.

More agreeable were the tennis matches on a court between the two consulates, although only two of the more active Russian ladies participated. Catherine was contemptuous about the concern of the remainder for their complexions as 'one could not play tennis and at the same time hold a sunshade up!'[96] The Macartneys clearly had much more time for the growing Swedish missionary colony, with their concern for the welfare of the local people, in particular their very popular medical services and educational work – it was so much easier to relax with people who spoke English; and they became very good friends.

Purdah parties for the European womenfolk were not uncommon later, and Diana Shipton records one which she herself hosted in Kashgar:

> There was no stiff silence and restraint. The room bulged with women; those who had no chair sat on the floor; everyone talked at once and screamed across to friends opposite; helpers picked their ways about with trays of cakes and tea, falling over crawling babies or bumping into each other, so that the tea poured into the carpet and cakes were trampled underfoot. The babies were being fed by their mothers or were howling, others chewed any available cake, ashtray and cigarette, or made a quiet pool to add to the general fun.[97]

Chini Bagh understandably became a home-from-home for visitors from every part of the world – scientists, surveyors, hunters, journalists and archaeologists. Two redoubtable British ladies, the Misses Kemp and MacDougal, courageously crossed the mountains via Ladakh and over the Karakorams shortly after the Revolution, despite Macartney's apprehensions. Catherine was more than pleased to have their company for several weeks, as she longed to have female English-speaking companionship: in her fourteen years at Chini Bagh, she met three only of her own countrywomen, and none in her first ten years there.

Because of the building of the new Consulate-General, guests had to be accommodated in large tents in the garden, and were quite happy with these. Catherine referred to one of these, Emily Georgiana Kemp, as a well-known artist and formidable traveller in Asia, but she did not mention that she was one of the first women students at Oxford. By a curious coincidence, Emily Kemp became a leading light in the World Congress of Faiths, of which Francis Younghusband, Catherine's own husband's first leader, was the founder and chairman. Kemp was perhaps characteristic of the assorted figures who passed through Kashgar over the years.

Captain Deasy, on his private surveying mission in 1900, was met by Macartney on his way to Kashgar and at Chini Bagh was overwhelmed by its relative comforts describing it as an 'oasis of civilisation …with an air of enchantment.' (He was especially grateful to Macartney for his efforts to overcome the suspicions of the Chinese about his surveying activities and his help in attempting to reach Tibet.) It was Deasy who gave an amusing illustration of Macartney's scrupulous observance of Chinese customs, when, at a funeral, Macartney surreptitiously checked from under his pith helmet whether the depth of his kow-tow was exactly that of the nearby Taotai.

Like all visitors, Ella Sykes was complimentary about her reception at Chini Bagh, even though she and her brother enjoyed the company of the Macartneys for only twenty-four hours before they left for England on leave. 'Lady Macartney gave us the kindest of greetings. Here it was so delightful to be once more in an English atmosphere and to talk to a countrywoman.'[98] At first we used to be accompanied on our walks and rides by Bielka and Brownie, the dogs that the Macartneys had left in our care…on our arrival Lady Macartney "introduced" us to him (Bielka was a large white wolf-like animal who disliked Europeans intensely) by providing us with bits of meat to give him as a peace offering and we became excellent friends.'[99]

In her *Daughters of Britannia*, which tells of the trials of diplomats' wives, Katie Hickman described part of the Sykes siblings' journey to Kashgar, as follows:

In 1915 an expedition to Kashgar, in Chinese Turkestan, was one of the most difficult journeys on earth. Following the outbreak of the First World War, the normal route for the first leg of the journey – across central Europe and down to the Caspian Sea – had become too dangerous, and so Ella and her brother Percy travelled to Petrograd (St Petersburg) on a vastly extended route via Norway, Sweden and Finland. From Petrograd they went south and east to Tashkent…on a train which lumbered its way through a slowly burgeoning spring…the train had no restaurant car, and the beleaguered passengers found it almost impossible to find food. At each halt, of which there were luckily three or four a day, they would all leap off the train and rush to buy what they could find at the buffets on the railway platforms, gulping down scalding bowls of cabbage soup or *borsch* in the few minutes that the train was stationary. The further east they travelled, the more meagre the food supplies became, until all they could procure was a kind of gritty Russian biscuit. Without the soup packets they had brought with them, Ella noted with some *sang froid*, they would have half starved.[100]

This was more or less the route which the Macartneys followed in reverse after the arrival of Ella and Percy Sykes, with the added complication of shepherding three children. Their first journey to Kashgar was under even more primitive conditions.

However, Ella's detailed descriptions of her travel experience complement those of Catherine. At night Ella and her brother stayed in rest houses, which in Russia usually consisted of a couple of small rooms, with bedsteads, a table and some stools. Sometimes these rooms looked out onto a courtyard where their ponies were tied for the night, but often there was no shelter either for the animals or their drivers. Over the border in China, these rooms became more rudimentary still, lit only by a hole in the roof. The walls were of crumbling mud, the ceilings unplastered, their beams the haunt of scorpions and tarantulas. Up in the mountains, of course, there were no lodgings of any kind.[101]

The rule was to rise at 5.00 a.m. if not earlier, wrote Ella:

….and I would hastily dress and then emerge from my tent to lay my pith-hat, putties, gloves and stick beside the breakfast table spread in the open. Diving back into my tent I would put the last touches to the packing of holdall and dressing-case, Jafar Bai and his colleague Humayun being busy meanwhile in tying up my bedstead and bedding. While the tents were being struck we ate our breakfast in the sharp morning air, adjusted our putties, applied face-cream to keep our skins from cracking in the intense dryness of the atmosphere, and then would watch our ponies, yaks or camels as the case might be, being loaded up.[102]

Most days they would walk for an hour or so before they took to their mounts. Ella usually rode side-saddle, but on these long journeys she found it less tiring to alternate with 'a native saddle', onto which she strapped a cushion They would march for five hours before taking lunch and a long rest in the middle of the day…when the worst of the midday heat was over, they would ride for another three or four hours. At high altitude – sometimes they were as high as 14,000 feet – she suffered from the extremes of temperature. During the day, beneath a merciless sun, in spite of her pith hat and sun-umbrella, she often felt as if she was being slowly roasted alive, while the nights were sometimes so cold that she was forced to wear every single garment she had with her, with a fur coat on top.'[103]

Recalling her own first journey across the mountains and subsequently, Catherine would of course have sympathised with all of this.

CHAPTER FIFTEEN

Tug-of-War

In the New Year's Honours List for 1913, Macartney was appointed as a Knight Commander of the Indian Empire after twenty-two years at Kashgar. While the new and much more prestigious consulate had been built at Chini Bagh, Macartney remained the modest tactful observer, renowned for keeping cool under pressure, but acting decisively when the occasion demanded. (Lady Macartney, as she now was, continued to be the cook for the family, in the absence of any other competent servant, and the controller of the domestic household.)

In the early part of that year, the remarkable English lady traveller, Miss E.G. Kemp, had stayed at the consulate for three weeks as indicated above. At Yarkand, she had found fifteen hundred British Indians who begged her to tell Sir Edward Grey that 'if it had not been for Sir G. Macartney, Russia would long ago have swallowed the whole country. The Chinese depend entirely on him for advice, and it has only been by his wise counsel that they have been prevented from giving the Russians the opportunity which they have been seeking of picking a quarrel.'[104] But she also mentioned that he was considerably disadvantaged in not having a Vice-Consul who could be sent to Yarkand and other places where there might be trouble, when the provincial capital at Urumchi was 800 miles away, requiring four months travel, which was out of the question. (Urumchi itself lies nearly 2,000 miles from China's east coast.)

The relationship with the Russians was altered by the appointment at Urumchi of the new Governor Yang Tseng-hsin, who with his powerful intellect and administrative ability, was to dominate the politics of the province for many years and brought a measure of stability after the earlier revolutions, although few Europeans, including Macartney, ever saw him. While elsewhere China was riven with factions, Xinjiang remained a relative haven of peace during Yang's seventeen years as governor. Much of this was achieved through his prestige among the Tungans, although he realised that this military force could be a double-edged sword. With this force behind him, he was able to thwart incipient plots and rebellions, while keeping the Russians at arm's length. For their part, they were still able to exploit any weaknesses in the British position.

This was made clear when they were able to complain to the British authorities, with some justification, that Macartney had encouraged the new Republican military governor in thinking that he could obtain modern arms with British support – which was seen as a possible Chinese threat to the Russians. (It provided an excuse for Sokov to increase his Cossack guard.) But the Chira trial dominated the politics of Xinjiang and became a battleground between the Russians, anxious to keep the Chinese, now flexing their muscles, in check: the Chinese themselves were concerned to retain their new-found independence in the face of Russian military power. This was all set against the background, notwithstanding Governor Yang's control, of a considerable breakdown of law and order in Kashgar and elsewhere, and a flouting of the authority of local officials. This also meant that Macartney's usual sources of information were truncated and he found difficulty in ascertaining what was going on.

Initially, the Chira trial in the spring of 1913 appeared to be going the way of the accused, and Sokov became increasingly agitated about the issue of the registration of locals as Russians, which the Chinese resented, while exaggerated reports of the Chira affair were sent back to St Petersburg. Macartney became caught up in this, as, without his permission, several Indian Aksakals (elders in their community) had also registered a number of traders as British subjects, actions which he had to disown. But he had difficulty in getting the British authorities to recognise the seriousness of the situation, with the Russians virtually threatening to annex Xinjiang, although this was not their real intention. Relations between the Russian Consul and the local Kashgar officials worsened, with Sokov becoming more belligerent over registration. At this point, Macartney reported:

> Kashgaria is now at the parting of the ways. Either it will remain what it was a year ago – namely a region where Russian influence, though preponderant, is not supported by military force, or it will follow the fate of North Manchuria – and that will be its fate if the Russian troops do not withdraw.[105]

(Outer Manchuria had been ceded by the Chinese as part of the Russian Empire by an obligatory treaty of 1860.)

Despite Russian denials that they intended to increase the force at Kashgar, the detachment there was increased to 1,000 cavalry and infantry by May 1913. The new Chinese military commander Titai Yang Tsuan-hus had previously been sent to Kashgar and seemed initially anxious to modernise his force. But even the threat of action by the Russians was enough to prompt Governor Yang Tseng-hsin to order the then Kashgar Titai, Chiao, to make an apology to the Russians. Nevertheless, the Chinese authorities were becoming increasingly intransigent. According to Macartney, this was less official policy than a general mood, following the revolution, of contempt for any authority, with the growing number of venal secret societies undermining the Chinese administration – a form of incipient anarchy. The situation was brought to a head when Chiao's successor, Titai Yang Tsuan-Hus, murdered his second-in-command, suspecting him of a plot to unseat him, just when Titai Yang Tsuan-hus had been instructed to sort out the Chira affair with the Russian consul. With a threat of mutiny by his troops, Yang Tsuan-hus had to barricade himself into his Headquarters and was only saved by the intervention of the veteran commander of the

The Diplomat of Kashgar   137

'Old Army' at Kashgar, Yang Hsietai. In due course Yang Tsuan-hus was removed from his post, as the Chinese bowed to Russian demands.

By the autumn of that year agreement had been reached on the Chira incident, with both Syed Haji and those who had burned down his father-in-law's house being quite severely punished alongside two district magistrates who had been shown to be incompetent over the whole affair. On the face of it, the Russians were victorious, but, significantly, Sokov did not pursue the nationality question which had caused so much grief, while the additional Russian troops left Kashgar when Sokov returned to St Petersburg.

Macartney was relieved that blood had not been spilt nor had the threatened annexation occurred. For this he could take some credit, as his messages and factual reports on Sokov's activities to the British Ambassador at St Petersburg had resulted in polite representations being made to the Foreign Ministry to good effect.

Macartney was still worried that the Russians might re-start registration. Particularly concerned that they might attempt to include Afghans, as this had not been legally prohibited, he made a six week tour of the southern oases, primarily to register British subjects, amounting to over 600. It says something for his trusted reputation that although the Chinese were becoming concerned about this activity, they allowed it, knowing that Macartney followed his own strict rules. Because of this, in 1914 he was appointed as Additional Assistant Judge of the British Supreme Court in the Shanghai Concession, with wide powers of registration. His reputation by now was such that the provincial governor, Yang Tseng-hsin, recommended him for a Chinese decoration, supported by the Kashgar officials who said 'The Hon-Consul-General has been a long time in Kashgar. His conciliatoriness and justice in the treatment of affairs are eulogised alike by officials, merchants, and ordinary people.'[106]

On his return to Kashgar towards the end of 1913, Macartney found Prince Mestchersky, who was both educated and inclined to be friendly, if not especially able, in the position of acting Russian Consul. Mestchersky was however anxious to avoid the confrontation of the Sokov era, particularly over the nationality question. By the spring of the following year, he was actually complaining to Macartney that he could not shift the Chinese from their bar on land purchase by Russians, or marriage to local Turki women, but more importantly, he could not get any support from his own government on the matter – a decided shift in official attitude.

In Kashgar, the gamblers were becoming even more powerful, flouting authority and appearing to be untouchable by the law. They controlled the appointed officials and encouraged opposition to the foreign consuls. But in February of 1914 they over-stepped the mark when they murdered an Amban. Governor Yang Tseng-hsin demonstrated his ruthlessness when he sent in his Muslim Tungan troops who dealt brutally with the gangs.

While Macartney was relieved to see the lawless elements 'sorted out' he felt obliged to report to his superiors:

> The question is how this policy adopted heretofore with success by the higher authorities in Urumchi, of playing off Muhammedan Dungans against Confucian Chinese will answer in the long run. So long as the former are well paid and given military commands, and so long as their coreligionists in the neighbouring province of Kansu remain quiescent, no disorder need be apprehended. None the less the Dungans are at present the controlling factor in the situation of the New Dominion; and the Chinese officials are, to a dangerous degree, dependent on their good will.[107]

With the withdrawal of the Peking subsidy, the economy of the province was in dire straits, not helped by a fifty per cent depreciation in currency value as a result of the indiscriminate issue of paper money, while the isolationist policies of Governor Yang Tseng-hsin pre-empted foreign investment. Trade with the Russians was greatly disrupted by the outbreak of World War I and Russian troops were progressively withdrawn from the frontier provinces – the Chinese welcomed the news of Russian defeats. There was a knock-on effect on British standing, being on the Russian side against the Germans. Before he went on leave in early 1915, Macartney was alarmed to hear that the German allies, the Turks, had sent five of their men to Kashgar with the intention of travelling to Afghanistan. He was in no doubt that their intention was to foment trouble there and even possibly to do likewise in India where there were nationalist movements against British rule. It was Macartney's temporary replacement, Sir Percy Sykes, who, with Prince Metschersky's help, persuaded the Chinese authorities to have the presumed *agents provacateurs* detained in Kashgar.

George and Catherine Macartney and staff on the verandah of Chini Bagh. Macartney wears a mourning arm-band presumably because of the recent death of Queen Victoria (22 January 1901). (LHAS)

CHAPTER SIXTEEN

A Challenging Journey

The Macartney family had intended, in order to start the children's education in England, to leave Kashgar in the summer of 1914, but the outbreak of war pre-empted that. Unfortunately, by this time they had not only sent off in advance all their heavy luggage, but also auctioned off many possessions. Meanwhile, the children's governess, Miss Cresswell, whose health had broken down, had already left for England, so that Catherine was left, not only with the usual round of domestic chores and cooking, made more difficult by the absence of stores from abroad due to the war, but also the older children's education, the youngest being only three. It is a reflection of the family's standing with the local community that the Kashgaris, when they realised the Macartneys' plight, returned all the auctioned goods so that they would not be bereft of their usual comforts in the meantime. All leave had been stopped with no indication of when they might depart.

At last word came through from India that a replacement in the form of Brigadier-General Sir Percy Sykes was on his way to relieve Macartney. All was bustle to get ready before the mountain passes were closed and in the midst of this, three-year-old Robin contracted fever, but recovered in time for the family to make a start. Catherine had a premonition that this was to be the last time she would see Chini Bagh, and despite the prospects of seeing home again, was sad at the thought. Because of the time of year, the thaw had set in and the mountain roads were slippery and dangerous, with stones and boulders bouncing down the hillsides.

The first her parents knew that their daughter Sylvia had been unseated by one of these rocks was when her riderless pony galloped past them, stampeding their own horses. When they got back to Sylvia, she was weeping with shock, although she and the servant were only slightly injured. When Macartney changed mounts with his daughter, another similar incident occurred and they realised that, through the melting of the ice high on the hillsides, boulders and rocks were detaching themselves from the slopes and hurtling down the hillsides at great speed, spooking the horses.

When they reached the first rest house, young Robin was badly burned by putting his hands on a red-hot stove and was in agony all night. To complicate matters, on the following day they found the road impassable for horses because of ice and the condition of the road. Catherine describes the scene:

> Dead and dying ponies, some horribly mutilated and injured, were lying all the way up, with their loads beside them, and vultures were hovering near, waiting till we had passed to begin their dreadful work.[108]

Sylvia and Robin were carried on the backs of two Kirghiz, while Catherine rode uncomfortably on the back of a floundering and continuously grunting yak. On foot, Macartney and Eric reached the summit with difficulty, but the boy collapsed at the top and could not be revived. Semi-conscious, he was put on a yak behind his mother and would have fallen off were it not for his mother's determination to keep hold of his hands around her waist, jolting down the precipitously steep gradient. At the foot, Eric was violently sick but to everyone's surprise and relief he immediately and completely recovered, obviously having suffered acute mountain sickness. However, a little further on, the horses began to show signs of nervousness. This was hardly surprising because soon the Macartneys came across a caravan of horses and men, the horses still standing but frozen to death, apparently caught in a blizzard, and the vultures were already at their work. The sight affected the whole family with a deep gloom, with Catherine especially unsure whether they would survive.

At Andijan, they were able to board the now familiar train in Russian Turkestan in temperatures which were a striking contrast to what they had experienced in the mountains, and encountered crowds of German prisoners-of-war. But at Orenburg, Cossacks boarded the train, drawing down the blinds and guarding all the carriage doors till they reached Samara, at the crossing of the Volga. Their journey and stopovers were made much more pleasant by the Tsar's ubiquitous prohibition on alcohol. They became aware of the war's effects when leaving Petrograd. Cossacks came aboard, drawing down the blinds with the threat that, if any were moved, the Cossacks on the line would shoot at the offending carriage, so great was their concern about spying on their fortifications near the Gulf of Finland. Someone on the train was actually shot through a window for this reason.

An unheralded military examination was an uncomfortable experience, when the whole family was virtually stripped and a message in one of Macartneys pockets written in Persian aroused the greatest suspicion – it was a fodder receipt and Macartney wisely suggested it be burnt. They were then asked to reveal any money or jewellery on their persons – in front of an officer with two revolvers in front of him on the table and flanked by Cossacks with fixed bayonets. Catherine was forced to hand over all her Russian currency and the English gold sovereigns she had sewn into her clothes. But when Macartney showed his official consular passport, the examining officer flew into a red rage, demanding to know why Macartney had not revealed his position before, as the officer would have been severely punished. According to Catherine, he literally threw their money back at them in his fury.

There were several more examinations to face before they reached the Finnish border. Because of the impossibility of crossing Germany, the family had been obliged to travel via Scandinavia, along with many other British people from China, Persia, and many parts of the east. They were entranced by the tranquil scenery of Finland and Sweden and the kindness of the people. At one point they faced crossing on foot over a frontier bridge where the icy, howling wind defeated the two younger children. A burly Swedish farmer popped them into his wheelbarrow for the crossing, whereupon the elderly Swedish toll-guard laughingly treated them as baggage and charged accordingly.

When it came to the medical examination, the doctor, hearing they had come from Kashgar, enquired if they knew his old friend Dr Sven Hedin. He had, as an explorer and archaeologist, became the doyen of Asiatic travel and had received the Macartney's famed hospitality. This was a good excuse for providing good coffee and friendly reminiscences of their mutual friend, despite Hedin's having become an apologist for Germany and its nationalistic aspirations. The final leg of their odyssey, between boarding at Bergen and Newcastle, was possibly the most dangerous, running the gauntlet of German mines, one of which came ominously close: an hour or two before a large vessel had been sunk off Aberdeen, while the boat on which the family travelled was torpedoed on her return voyage. Catherine had wept quietly on the family's arrival at the Newcastle quayside. She was not to know then that her proposal to return to Kashgar after six months was precluded by a ban on women travelling at that time, and she was obliged subsequently to say farewell to her husband to finish his last three years of service on his own, retracing the steps they had taken across Europe.

In August 1915, on the basis of the wartime alliance with Russia, Macartney had drawn up a detailed memorandum on how the two countries could cooperate in defining their spheres of influence. This involved the Russians recognising British interests in Hunza, Raskam and the Taghdumbash Pamirs, and in return Britain would promise not to seek any interest in the province north of the Tien Shan. There were also reciprocal agreements on trading taxation. Not surprisingly, with a desperate war on, the British Government ignored the memorandum.

When, after his leave in England, Macartney returned in November 1915, he found a splendid consulate-general; but without his family, what must have been his sense of desolation! While relations with the Russians had vastly improved, the Chinese authorities were increasingly hostile to foreigners in their land and their presumed rights which the Chinese not unnaturally wished to reclaim. Because of the wartime alliance with Russia, British status was being eroded, although Macartney tried to persuade the Chinese that Germany was also a potential enemy to them, especially with their capacity to foment trouble with the Muslim population.

Meanwhile, the Tungan power was growing in the province – the new Tungan Titai, Ma Fuh-hsing, had brought to Kashgar some three thousand conscripted levies. With the appointment of a Tungan District Magistrate, they were now a power in the land and showed this by their unopposed summary execution without trial of those Chinese deemed to be members of secret societies. Macartney described the Tungan troops as 'undisciplined, ignorant and ferocious' and was concerned that other Muslims might attach themselves to this force. The new régime in Peking and elsewhere seemed to be following in the footsteps of the Manchus in their arbitrary exercise of power and dismissal of any democratic system of government. In Kashgar, anyone espousing republicanism was liable to be shot out of hand. Yuan Shih-k'ai even reverted to the Manchu title of Emperor in January 1916, while elsewhere, the Provincial Governors ruled by a mailed fist, not least in Xinjiang, although increasingly dependent on Tungan military backing.

In Kashgar, a rift deepened between the military commander and the xenophobic Taotai, each trying to recruit the British and Russian consuls as allies. The tug-of-war was largely over the rights of foreign nationals to purchase land. The Taotai forbade this by proclamation, but was over-ruled by the Provincial Governor in Urumchi, and the Taotai was eventually dismissed. Taking his lead from his superior, the Titai [*sic*] or military commander was more cooperative towards the consuls and overt opposition to them faded away.

However, Governor Tseng-hsin Yang clearly showed his ruthlessness when he invited a number of officers from Yunnan to dinner and had them shot one by one on suspicion of agitating for an independent Xinjiang to complement the rebellion in Yunnan province. He then resumed his dinner. Yang himself was to meet a similar fate when he was assassinated in 1928. China was obviously in a very feeble state with overlords using extreme violence and corruption to maintain their personal positions. Referring to the men in power, Macartney reported:

> ...anyone, be his political creed what it may, who attempts to disturb them, they will seize and summarily shoot down. At present, the Governor and the Titai wield extraordinary powers; and I doubt if any Chinese authority, not even that from Peking, can remove them, barring the one derived from the knife of the assassin. For the moment Xinjiang appears to stand as a self-contained entity.[109]

CHAPTER SEVENTEEN

Tashkent Mission

In June 1916 the Emperor Yuan Shih-k'ai died, but this made little difference to the situation in Xinjiang, since Governor Tseng-hsin Yang had always shown at least nominal allegiance to his masters in Peking. What he did not wish was that either the Russians or the Chinese should show any interest in the province which he ruled. He did however recognise that the increasing Turki nationalism could pose a threat and he was therefore wary of any German or Turkish attempts to encourage this. He was intelligent enough to realise that he had to make some concessions to the Muslim population. For example, he allowed the re-opening of schools in Kashgar, but simultaneously insisted that the schools' curriculum and activities include Chinese military drill and the learning of the Chinese language. This effectively reduced the school roll to half of what it had been.

However, Macartney became alarmed by the progressive penetration of German and Muslim agents into Kashgaria, especially their encouragement of the anti-British elements referred to above, amongst the Afghan population, both in Xinjiang and in Afghanistan itself. It became clear that the German intention was to unite the Muslims under the banner of the Pan-Islamic movement to undermine British authority. This was perceived as a real threat to British India; but Macartney was up against the declared neutrality of China when he sought action against these elements, either by arrest or deportation to inner China. One of the most blatant incursions was that led by the German officer Von Hentig who had left Germany with a considerable entourage and entered Afghanistan. Although received politely by the Amir, the latter was cunning enough not to commit to either the German or the British side until he knew which would win the great contest. Frustrated, Von Hentig made his way into Xinjiang, where at Yarkand in the summer of 1916, he more or less openly began intriguing with the Afghans there.

What happened next had elements of both drama and farce. Macartney and Mestchersky combined in their efforts to persuade the Chinese authorities to remove the Germans to inner China, thus cutting them off from the province's Afghan population. Again, the Taoyin played the neutrality card, while Macartney sought approval from Peking for Von Hentig's removal. The German officer made it clear to Macartney that he was not going to be intimidated, while offering to meet him in Kashgar. The Chinese refused to use force against Von Hentig, who simply sat tight. The issue was a serious one, which could cast doubt in the Chinese official mind as to how far the Afghans were under British protection. A complicating factor was that several Swedish missionaries were sympathetic to the German cause and their mission might easily provide a sanctuary for the Germans who were claiming that Turks, Afghans, Wakhanis, Persians and others were under German jurisdiction and that they were intervening with the Chinese authorities on their behalf.

Despite a control order, Von Hentig succeeded in escaping from Yarkand and making his way, with several accomplices, to Kashgar. Macartney got to know about this when the Germans were virtually at the gates of the city. Fearing an attack on the Consulate-General, he was able to secure a guard of five Cossacks and simultaneously prompted the local military commander to send out immediately his whole contingent of troops to stop the 'invaders.' The subsequent confrontation, with each side threatening to open fire on the other, ended when Von Hentig allowed himself to be taken to the *yamen* where he was obliged to remain for a week under a guard of a hundred Chinese soldiers. The upshot, after much deliberation and consultation between the consuls and the Chinese, was that the German party, under the strongest protests, were deported to inner China under a formidable guard.

Another attempt at infiltration in September 1916 was made when two men, claiming to be Norwegian mining engineers and who spoke Chinese well, arrived in Khotan. When they left for the Raskam Valley to the south, Macartney became suspicious, and even more so when a telegram to the Norwegian Minister in Peking revealed that he knew nothing of them. Macartney promptly arranged for the dispatch of some Hunza Scouts to intercept them. Describing the so-called engineers ironically, 'as on the benevolent mission of scattering gold sovereigns among the Afghans and of instructing these people the way they should go,' Macartney stated that 'the Hunza men pretended to be Afghan soldiers...and the Scouts undertook to act as guides leading them into Gilgit and into the arms of the British representative there.'[110] At Gilgit, one of the 'engineers' was found to be the Secretary of the German Legation in Peking. Macartney became increasingly concerned that fresh parties of Germans might even yet be sent by Von Hentig in the east into the province and thence into Afghanistan or even stay in Kashgaria to foment trouble there. It was known that the Germans had some Chinese sympathisers who, for their own reasons, might well assist them.

The unusual action of Macartney in obtaining this military presence to patrol the Kukturuk Valley on the route into Afghanistan to stop such infiltration was one which might have resulted in a serious diplomatic row, given that this was Chinese territory. Fortunately, Yang Taoyin, who had furiously demanded an explanation, was dismissed by the Governor before he appointed a replacement, Chu, in March 1917. He was much more inclined to cooperate with the foreign consuls, more especially when, on 21 August, China declared war on Germany. The reasons for this were several, but prominent among these was China's desire to secure its position, and in particular to have a seat at the table when the Great Powers were making post-war decisions on the division of spoils. Chu lost no time in rounding up any Turks in Kashgaria, while the Governor put a stop to the illicit export of arms to Afghanistan.

With the advent of the Russian Revolution in 1917, the British authorities faced a new situation. The Bolsheviks sought to overcome White Russian Tsarist forces in a barbaric struggle for supremacy. Having up to this point been considered a friendly ally, Britain was now regarded, especially by the more conservative Russian establishment, with some suspicion. That suspicion was mutual, especially when it became known that the Bolsheviks were now intent on exporting their brand of Communism world-wide, including to India, Afghanistan, the Middle and Far East. This campaign was intended to help conquer the West by undermining the imperial economies through strikes and insurrection by nationalists, and it all started in Central Asia, at a time when there was a virtual absence of organised government there.

Meanwhile, the Germans were also stirring up trouble among the frontier tribes. With the threat of a combined German and Turkish advance on Afghanistan in particular, Britain needed, through its Secret Service agents, to obtain information on the strength and attitudes of the Soviets along the southern Russian border, centred on Tashkent, now under Bolshevik rule. In particular, they sought information as to who was likely to be the victor between the Tsarist forces and the Bolsheviks. (Tashkent was identified as the base for a school of Bolshevik propaganda especially directed towards India.) Part of the plan was to keep the Germans out of Central Asia by any possible means: From Meshed, Lieut-Col. Ernest Redle had instructions to blow up the Transcaspian Railway to deny it to the German-Turkish forces. It was another 'Great Game'.

It was decided to send a mission to the new Russian authorities there, and Macartney was appointed guide and interpreter. The other members of the mission sent ahead of Macartney were two army officers, Col. F. M Bailey and Captain Stewart Blacker, while another officer, Major Percy Etherton, was appointed to maintain the listening post at the Consulate-General in Kashgar. On the way to Kashgar, Bailey's Mission was greeted with a great fanfare of banners and trumpets, and even given a hearty reception by the Russian consul Strephanovitch, including dancing to a gramophone.[111] Blacker arrived on a Triumph motor cycle brought over the mountains from India. This caused something of a sensation as the first motorised transport seen in Kashgar, and he rode this machine part of the way to Tashkent.[112] All three spent several weeks in Kashgar while Macartney made preparations for handing over and his final return to England.

At his leaving Kashgar on 11 August 1918, all of the British subjects, the whole Russian colony, the Swedes and the Chinese gathered *en masse* to bid him farewell. Etherton recorded in his official diary: 'It would be difficult to imagine more genuine cordiality and esteem than that displayed on Sir George's departure, and it testifies to the extraordinary influence and popularity he had acquired.'

Later, in a letter to the *The Times* in November 1922, Captain Blacker wrote concerning Macartney's part in the Tashkent Mission: 'Sir George's modesty prevents him from making clear that it was his personality, his knowledge, his experience of Turkestan, and his prestige with the Soviet that made him the unquestioned head of the Mission in Tashkent.'[113]

Macartney was well known in Tashkent which he had visited on several occasions during his career. Blacker might have added that Macartney may well have been responsible for the escape of both officers from Tashkent in one piece, as he himself said: 'I had visions of the interior of a Bolshevik gaol' after a particularly tense encounter with Kolosov, the President of the new Bolshevik Republic. (The latter had ordered a massacre in Kokand against a rebellion of Muslims in which many thousands had been killed under the most brutal circumstances.) Macartney claimed that 'it was just touch and go that they [Bailey and Blacker] were not arrested forthwith as spies' before his own arrival at Tashkent. On the way through the mountains to the railhead he became aware of 'a gang of some sixty armed robbers... looting the Kirghiz and carrying off their women. They however, took no notice of my caravan.'[114]

He himself had a rough rail journey to Tashkent: describing the rush to get on the train 'when everyone scrambled in as best he could, some through the doors and others through the windows and as the inside of the carriages became choke-full [*sic*], a dense mass of humanity invaded the carriage roofs on which they stood or squatted. Even the roofs of the carriages were crammed with passengers. Through a lavish distribution of bribes...I secured a coupé for myself, my two servants, and my baggage.' At this point a woman forced herself into the space. Claiming to be the wife of the Commissary of all the railways in Turkistan, she roundly berated Macartney as a bourgeois and threatened to have him, his servants, and his baggage thrown on the lines. Ever the diplomat, Macartney subsequently obtained for her some hot water for her tea, when she not only calmed down, but revealed much about the situation in Tashkent and the startling news that British Indian troops were now in Askabad, which Macartney knew boded ill for the mission. Macartney then spent the night on the floor of the station waiting-room at Tashkent fearing for his safety if he was found abroad at that hour.[115]

In Tashkent, Macartney had been summoned on 1 September to explain the purpose of the British Mission. In the middle of their interview, Kolosov dropped a bombshell: he let the Mission know of the landing of British troops and arms, including tanks and guns, at

Archangel, on behalf of the Tsarist forces – this, the British agents in Tashkent knew nothing about. The Bolsheviks may have held their hand against the Mission in the hope of British support or at least recognition; or possibly because the revolutionaries had plans to bolt back to Kashgar if things went wrong, which was not unlikely.

The British officers were skating on the thinnest of ice. Etherton described the Bolsheviks as 'ruthless fanatics', which many were, and wrote that 'one false step, and the lives of the mission would not have been worth a moment's purchase.' Fortunately, Kolosov indicated that he required instructions from Moscow.[116] Suspected spies and any who opposed the regime were being executed out of hand. Macartney had anticipated that the Mission might be put in gaol or even face a firing squad. In fact, the Mission's situation in Tashkent was extremely dangerous, to say the least. The local Bolshevik newspaper poured scorn on the British objectives and demanded a truthful explanation. One of the more extreme Soviet factions, the Red Guards, demanded that the Mission be arrested forthwith as spies. Members of the Mission were followed everywhere and there were even attempts to trap them by using *agents provocateurs*. Macartney was subjected to a fierce cross-examination by the chief commissar as to how the British could reconcile their recent landing at Archangel to support the Tsarist regime with an ostensibly friendly Mission to Tashkent. The British officers, asking about the cries and rifle shots at night near to their hotel, were not encouraged by the explanation that the Bolsheviks were merely making room in the over-crowded gaol by shooting surplus prisoners! An attempt on Lenin's life on 30 August, thought to be the work of a British agent, greatly increased Russian suspicions. Blacker, who fell ill with an unidentified malady, decided to accompany Macartney to India and they crossed the border just in time, having been trailed everywhere in Tashkent. The news came through of the execution of twenty-four Bolshevik Commissars at Baku by the White Russians on

20 September, at which it was claimed British army officers were present.[117]

As the most active of the British agents under Sir Wilfrid Malleson, who ran a network of spies from Meshed in north-east Persia, Col. F.M. Bailey was a marked man and had astonishing adventures as a master of disguise: he even succeeded in convincing the notorious Russian Secret Service, the Cheka, to employ him to track himself down! His hair-breadth escapes from his hunters became legendary. Of Macartney, he said, 'His influence and support proved invaluable to Blacker and me.'[118] A note by "A.C.Y.", the Editor of the Journal in question, on Macartney's paper on Bolshevism delivered to the Central Asian Society in 1920, states that 'Until it was known that Lieutenant-Colonel F.M. Bailey was out of reach of Bolshevist animosity, it was not deemed wise or right to publish this lecture.' At this event, Sir Percy Sykes stated that, 'Although Sir George Macartney had been very modest in his reference to the risks he had run, they could not help realising how appalling these risks had been. Those of them who had been in these parts knew very well the extraordinary risks that had been run....'[119]

Meanwhile, at Kashgar, Etherton ran his anti-Bolshevik campaign as if it was a personal vendetta. He built up a network of agents, sending a stream of intelligence back to London. By January 1918 he had a wireless receiving set able to intercept Bolshevik messages between Tashkent and Moscow. At Kashgar he had a Vice-Consul, British wireless monitors, a chief clerk, an assistant clerk, a Chinese secretary and numerous orderlies and servants plus an escort of forty sepoys commanded by an Indian officer.[120]

Skrine records that because of the situation in Russia after the Tashkent Mission, Macartney had to retrace his steps and ride back to Sarikol and Gilgit to return home via India and comments:

It was typical of the many ironies of his career that while he was making his way to the Indian border there arrived on 22 September the first British troops to be seen in Kashgar. For twenty-eight years Macartney had protected British interests in Xinjiang through all kinds of dangerous situations without the help of a single soldier. Now when he was leaving behind him an impressive Consulate-General, and an unquestioned position for his successor, in a Kashgar where Russian influence had ceased to exist and where order was kept by the strong hand of Governor [Tseng-hsin] Yang, who effectively kept the Bolsheviks out of Xinjiang, a British consular guard arrived from India, while the man who for so many years had been denied its support slipped away quietly into retirement.[121]

Macartney retired with his family to Jersey where he appears to have led a very quiet life apart from writing the occasional paper on Xinjiang and giving talks. One of these greatly upset Cotterell Tupp, the original proposer of the Central Asian Society, which was firmly in favour of an aggressive policy in the empty spaces between the Indian and Russian empires. This was because Macartney had admitted that a British retreat would be inevitable if the Russians invaded Xinjiang.[122]

The Channel Islands, including Jersey, were occupied by the Germans during World War II, the only part of the British Isles to be invaded. (The British Government decided that the islands would not be defended.) The German occupation served no military purpose, other than for propaganda. The majority of the Jersey Islanders, anticipating the invasion, chose to stay on the island and many were active in resistance to the invaders. Some were sent to prison camps in Europe. Many islanders provided shelter for fugitives from the Nazi regime in Europe and forced labourers employed on the islands. In 1942, the Germans announced that all residents of the Channel Islands who were not born there were to be deported – in

Jersey twenty-two islanders died in concentration camps.[123]

During the German occupation, Macartney himself was under a real threat of deportation to Germany, but this was possibly averted by his long illness. He died on 19 May 1945, a few days after the occupation ended. His brother Donald, who had been with the family at Chini Bagh during the Chinese revolution, had been killed long before, in 1918, while fighting with his Canadian regiment. Catherine survived her husband by four years, dying in Charminster, Dorset, in 1949.

Sir George Macartney with his wife and three children, Les Vaux, Jersey, 19 September 1920. (LHAS)

The Diplomat of Kashgar 156

CHAPTER EIGHTEEN

A Very Special Agent

'The record of George Macartney's career in Sinkiang is one of a remarkable personal achievement. Few men could have succeeded as he did in representing British interests, almost unsupported and in the face of determined opposition, for twenty-eight years in one of the most inaccessible posts in the service of the British government. His ability and courage were matched by his modesty, which concealed his achievements from all but a few government officials and travellers who read his reports or benefitted from his advice.'[124]

So said Sir Clarmont Skrine at the end of his book, *Macartney at Kashgar*. Skrine goes on to emphasise that Macartney's success was achieved despite the lack of a consistent British policy for Xinjiang, which meant that the consul was obliged to formulate his own policy, with the added difficulty that the British and Indian Governments failed to keep him informed about important changes. Macartney's position in Kashgar was always under threat from the bullying Russians or vacillating Chinese.

Without official status or support for many years, Macartney achieved important objectives. Among these, the most important were his protection of the interests of British traders in the face of Russian commercial privileges and perhaps above all, the freeing of British Indian slaves. Through his official observations and reports which reached St Petersburg, he was able to restrain the more aggressive intentions of the Russians, while providing wise advice, through his tact and diplomatic skills, to the Chinese, who were often bewildered by events. In all of this he was greatly supported by a courageous and adaptable wife in a happy family life.

Although the Anglo-Soviet Convention of 1907 had officially ended almost a century of Anglo-Soviet rivalry in this frontier area, the continuing power of Russia in the region continued to be of concern to the British imperial administration. Following the First World War, the Russian revolution of 1917, and the subsequent creation of Soviet Socialist Republics, there was increasing concern in the British Government regarding the infiltration throughout the British Empire of communist and nationalist agents and ideas. A form of the 'Great Game' was resurrected with spies, intelligence officers and adventurers foraging for information in the high plateaus of Central Asia and Xinjiang in particular. A Russian invasion of Western China in 1934, in which White Russians and the Red Army combined, led to Russia dominating Xinjiang. The province was virtually cut off from the rest of the country for most of the decade, during which time there were many uprisings. However, by the mid-1950s, Soviet influence had come to an end.

Now, in the 21st Century, there is considerable interest in the economies, geopolitics, and history of former Soviet Central Asian republics such as Kazakhstan, Uzbekistan, Kyrgystan, Tajikistan and Turkmenistan. Much essential historic information can be found in the reports of officials such as Macartney in the archives of the Political and Secret Department of the India Office and of the India Office Military Department (now in the British Library in London). China is now much concerned to maintain stability and control over peripheral territories such as Tibet and Xinjiang in the face of increasingly nationalistic ethnic communities such as the Uyghur. From a population of two million in the 1930s, this has risen to over twenty million. But there is Uyghur resentment against the increasing migration of Han Chinese into the Province and their occupation of the higher posts, while the Chinese are often contemptuous of the easy-going Uyghurs and their distinctive culture. Kashgar's modern thriving tourist industry may be compromised by China's recent attempts to 'modernise' its famous Old City.

In 1949, the Han Chinese population was 6.7% of the total. This has now risen to a staggering 40%. Violence erupted in the 1990s and as many as two hundred people were killed in one incident alone: in February 2012, Muslim activists killed twelve people in Kashgar. As recently as March 2013, twenty people were sentenced in Kashgar to a maximum prison term of life, on charges of separatism and plotting to carry out jihad in Xinjiang. China is very much aware that the province has borders with five Muslim-dominated countries, including Pakistan and Afghanistan. It has attempted to recruit the support of both western and other Central Asian states, such as Kazakhstan, Tajikistan, Turkmenistan, and Uzbekistan, by claiming these riots are linked to Muslim fundamentalists and Al-Qaeda. China has designated Western Xinjiang as a special economic zone and a transport hub, with massive infrastructural investment, including the recent completion of a railway connection between Khotan and Kashgar. Anything resembling organised dissent against the prevailing central (Chinese) authority is quickly – and often ruthlessly – suppressed. The Chinese are apparently determined to retain control over their Muslim Uyghur subjects. In some important respects therefore, things have not changed significantly since George Macartney's day.

'A very, parfit gentil knight'[125]

APPENDIX

Titles of Officials within the Provincial Administration in China in the 19th and Early 20th Centuries

Aksakal or Aqsaqal: local headman (of village) and local magistrate sometimes representative of a group of British Indian traders.

Amban: Representative of Chinese Government above Taoyin and the magistrate in charge of one of the forty-five districts in the Province (equivalent to a Collector or District Officer in India)

Titai: Military Provincial Commander- in- Chief.

Taotai: District Magistrate and honorific title for Taoyin above.

Taoyin: head of civil and military affairs in a circuit (i.e. two or more territorial departments) and local magistrate who was the Governor's representative, appointed by the latter, and presiding over one of the six circuits making up the Province of Xinjiang responsible for administration, supervising customs and collection of revenue (the equivalent of a British colonial district commissioner).

REFERENCES

Bailey, F.M. (2002) *Mission to Tashkent*. Oxford University Press.

Boulger, D.C. (1908) *The Life of Sir Halliday Macartney*. London & New York. John Lane.

Cable, Mildred & Francesca French (1942) *The Gobi Desert*. London. Hodder & Stoughton.

Cruikshank, C.G. (1975) *The German Occupation of the Channel Islands*. London. OUP.

Dalrymple, W. (1990) *In Xanadu: A Quest*. London. Fontana.

Deasy, H.H.H. (1901) *In Tibet and Chinese Turkestan*. London. T. Fisher Unwin.

Elias, N. (1886) *Report of a Mission to Chinese Turkestan and Badakhan in 1885-86*. Vol. V, Part I. Mss Eur 112/376. Calcutta. Printed by the Superintendent of Government Printing, India.

Ellis, C.H. (1963) *The British Intervention in Transcaspia*. London. Hutchinson & Co.

Etherton, P.T. (1925) *In the Heart of Asia*. London. Constable & Co.

Ewans, M. ed. (2008) *Britain and Russia in Central Asia 1880-1907*. London. Routledge.

Frazer, M.D. ed. (1907) *Marches of Hindustan: The Record of a Journey in Tibet, Trans-Himalayan India, Chinese Turkestan, Russian Turkestan and Persia*. Edinburgh and London. Wm. Blackwood and Sons.

French, P. (1994) *Younghusband: The Last Great Imperial Adventurer*. London. Harper Collins.

Genovese, Lia. (2006) *Proceedings (Extract) of XII International Congress of Orientalists, Rome, October 1899*. Translation and analysis. http://idp.bl.uk/4DCGI/education/orientalists/index.a4d

Hickman, K. (1999) *Daughters of Britannia: The Lives and Times of Diplomatic Wives.* London. Harper Collins.

Hopkirk, P. (1980) *Foreign Devils on the Silk Road: The Search for the Lost Cities and Treasures of Chinese Central.* London. Asia Oxford University Press & John Murray.

_____ (1984) *Setting the East Ablaze*: *Lenin's Dream of an Empire in Asia.* London. John Murray.

_____ (1991) *Great Game: On Secret Service in High Asia.* Oxford, UK. OUP.

Jha, P.K. (1985) *History of Sikkim, 1817-1904: Analysis of British Policy and Activities.* Calcutta. O.P.S.

Jones, R.A. (1983) *The British Diplomatic Service 1815-1914.* Gerards Cross, London. Colin Smythe.

Lamb, A. (1960) *Britain and Chinese Central Asia: the Road to Lhasa, 1767-1905.* London. Routledge and Kegan Paul.

Macartney, C.T. (1931) *An English Lady in Chinese Turkestan.* London. Ernest Benn.

Macartney, G. (1920) 'Bolshevism as I saw it at Tashkent in 1918'. London. *J. Roy. Central Asian Society, 7, 1920, 42-55.*

MacDonald, C. (1900) *Report on the Boxer Rebellion: Siege of the Peking Embassy.* London. Her Majesty's Stationery Office, 2000.

Mayer, K.E. & Brysac, S.B. (2001) *Tournament of shadows: the great game and the race for empire in Asia.* London. Abacus.

Michie, A. (1900) *The Englishman in China during the Victorian era, as illustrated in the career of Sir Rutherford Alcock, etc.* 2 vols. London. William Blackwood & Sons.

Millward, J.A. (1985) *Eurasian Crossroads: A History of Xinjiang.* Hong Kong. Oxford University Press.

Mirsky, J. (1977) *Sir Aurel Stein: Archaeological Explorer.* Chicago. University of Chicago Press.

O'Connor, R. (1974). *The Boxer Rebellion.* London. Robert Hale.

Satow, E.M. (1917) *Guide to diplomatic practice.* 2 vols. London. Longman Green & Co.

Skrine, C.P. (1986) *Chinese Central Asia: An Account of Travels in Northern Kashmir and Chinese Turkestan.* Hong Kong and Oxford. OUP.

Skrine, C.P. & Nightingale, P.M. (1973) *Macartney at Kashgar.* London. Methuen & Co.

Stein, M.A., Sir (1903) *Sand-buried ruins of Khotan: Personal narrative of a journey of archaeological and geographical exploration.* London.

Sykes, E.C. and Brig.-General Sir Percy M. Sykes (1920) *Through Deserts and Oases of Central Asia.* London. Macmillan.

Tuson, P. ed. (2005) *British Intelligence on Russia in Central Asia, c. 1865-1949.* London. IDC Publishers.

Warikoo, K. ed. (2009) *Himalayan Frontiers of India: Historical, Geopolitical and Strategic.* London. Routledge Contemporary South Asia.

Wu, Aitchen K. (1984) *Turkistan Tumult.* Hong Kong. OUP.

Younghusband, F.E. (1984) *Heart of a Continent: A narrative of Travels in Manchuria, across the Gobi Desert, Through the Himalayas, the Pamirs, and Chitral, 1884-1894.* Hong Kong and New York. OUP.

NOTES

[1] Answer to a query from an unknown person to the Government of India, Foreign Department, Calcutta National Archives of India, Frontier B, April 1901, No. 383.

[2] Mirsky, 134.

[3] This family association went even further when George Macartney's only sister Alice married James W. Borland, son of Sir Halliday Macartney's old friend of the same name.

[4] 'Chinese' Gordon was later to become the celebrated martyr of the defence of Khartoum, when after his murder, his own head was paraded by the Mahdi, who, by a strange quirk of fate, was said to have ordered his own officers not to kill the British general.

[5] Boulger, 136.

[6] Boulger, 140.

[7] Boulger, 140-43.

[8] Jones, 227, Appendix C.

[9] Jones, 140-144.

[10] Satow, 183-84.

[11] Skrine & Nightingale, 3.

[12] Lamb, 183-84.

[13] As in the sub-title to French, P. (1994).

[14] Warikoo, viii.

[15] FY155, Younghusband Collection in the India Office Library (Mss. EUR F197/), now held in the British Library, quoted in P. French (1994), 83.

[16] Elias, Vol. 5, Part I. The Forsyth Mission, named after its leader, had been sent in 1873 to conclude a trade treaty with the Amir of Yarkand and Kashgar, Ya'qub Beg, and also to gather intelligence on the area.

[17] Taotai: An honorific for the position of Taoyin i.e. the Governor's representative, appointed by the latter, and presiding over one of the six circuits making up the Province of Xinjiang and responsible for administration, supervising customs and collection of revenue – the equivalent of a British colonial district commissioner.

[18] French, P., 87.

[19] Hopkirk, 463-64.

[20] Dalrymple, 322.

[21] Younghusband Collection, FY 155, India Office Library (mss. Eur 197/). Quoted in French, P. (1994), 83.

[22] *Ibid*, FY/219, French, P. (1994), 103.

[23] Stein, 111-113.

[24] Cable, 293.

[25] See Titles of Officials within the provincial administration in China in 19th and early 20th centuries, below.

[26] Macartney, Catherine, 115.

[27] Cable, 70.

[28] Skrine, 51.

[29] Cable, 167-68.

[30] Millward, 162.

[31] Mirsky, 138.

[32] Dalrymple, 227.

[33] Skrine & Nightingale, 102ff.

[34] Fraser, 229.

[35] It is unlikely that Macartney would have prescribed imprisonment if he had known anything about the barbarous conditions of Chinese jails at the time when inmates often begged for beheading to end their sufferings.

[36] Fraser, 269.

[37] "Indian traders" were also "Hindu tenants" in this context.

[38] Amban: The magistrate in charge of one of the forty-five districts in the Province; equivalent to a Collector or District Officer in India and the commander-in-chief of that area.

[39] Michie, 362-67.

[40] Skrine & Nightingale, 62.

[41] *Ibid.*, 63.

[42] *Ibid.*, 63.

[43] *Ibid.*, 64.

[44] *Ibid.*, 70.

[45] *Ibid.*, 83.

[46] *Ibid.*, 84.

[47] One writer refers to the Macartneys coming home on leave to Edinburgh, but this author could find no confirmation of this.

[48] Skrine & Nightingale, 97.

[49] Macartney, C., 2.

[50] Skrine & Nightingale, 111.

[51] O'Connor, R., 219-220.

[52] This soldier-diplomat gave his name to the Macartney-Macdonald Line, demarcating the Chinese-Indian Border at Aksai Chin.

[53] MacDonald, 286.

[54] Macartney, C., 56-57.

[55] Hopkirk (1980), 49.

[56] Genovese, 1.

[57] Mirsky, 79-81.

[58] Companion of the Order of the Indian Empire.

[59] Stein, xxi.

[60] Macartney, G., 234-43.

[61] Macartney, G., 283-85.

[62] Stein, 120.

[63] *Ibid.*, 121-26.

[64] *Ibid.*, 126-27.

[65] Mirsky, 133.

[66] *Ibid.*, 135.

[67] *Ibid*, 137.

[68] *Ibid.*, 141.

[69] Stein, 457-58. The wooden collar is usually referred to as "the cangue".

[70] Cable & French, 46-7.

[71] Mirsky, 230.

[72] *Ibid.*, 491.

[73] Macartney, G., 234-43.

[74] Some apologists have claimed – certainly with some justification – that this removal may have saved objects and manuscripts from being overcome by the shifting desert sands or taken by treasure hunters for pecuniary gain, which could not have been said of the archaeologists. On a later expedition Stein removed some eleven large panels of Buddhist frescoes.

[75] For further information, see Stein, *Ruins of Desert Cathay* (2 vols), Vol. 1, 107-8.

[76] Mirsky, 234.

[77] Stein to Allen, 9 Oct 1913 (MS in Allen file, Bodleian Library), as quoted by Mirsky, 360, 362.

[78] Mirsky, 362.

[79] *Ibid.*, 364.

[80] *Orientalia Josephi Tucci memoriae dicata.* Vol. I, Instituto italiano per il Medio ed Estremo oriente 1985, 168.

[81] *Sic* for "Witness". NB the author was not a native English speaker.

[82] Genovese, 'Summary and Conclusions', 7.

[83] If Macartney had read Satow later he would have found that written instructions for diplomats were not always available and that '...the usual practice is to inform him (the incoming diplomat) that in the archives of his mission he will find most of the instructions he needs, and that others will reach him from time to time.' Satow was referring to established diplomatic posts. (Satow, 201)

[84] Skrine & Nightingale, 120.

[85] *Ibid.*, 128.

[86] "Gardening soldiers": Known to the European community by this term as the soldiers apparently spent far more time in this activity than military training.

[87] Skrine & Nightingale, 176.

[88] Rev. George W. Hunter travelled widely in Xinjiang as an itinerant missionary with the China Inland Mission and translated much of the Bible into Kazakh in addition to his English translations of Turkic literature. He was imprisoned on false charges and tortured over thirteen months by the Soviet authorities in Urumchi after the Bolshevik revolution.

[89] Macartney, C., 185.

[90] Macartney, C., 186.

[91] *Ibid.*, 186-7.

[92] *Ibid.*, 187.

[93] *Ibid.*, 190.

[94] *Ibid.*, 192.

[95] Sykes, 42.

[96] Macartney, C., 208.

[97] Hickman, 167.

[98] Sykes, 38.

[99] *Ibid.*, 54.

[100] Hickman, 2.

[101] Based on Hickman, 3.

[102] Ella, as quoted by Hickman, 4.

[103] This is the author's summary of what Hickman tells us about Ella. (Hickman, 5.)

[104] Skrine & Nightingale, 209.

[105] *Ibid.*, 223.

[106] *Ibid.*, 234.

[107] *Ibid.*, 236.

[108] Macartney, C., 221.

[109] Skrine & Nightingale, 247.

[110] Macartney, G. (1920) 45-6.

[111] Hopkirk (1984), 21.

[112] Etherton, 95.

[113] Blacker and Bailey had left Kashgar for Tashkent on 24 July 1918, accompanied by Stephanovich, Secretary of the Russian Consulate General, to smooth their path by acting as interpreter. Remarkably, the Mission passed without difficulty through Irkishtan, Osh, and Andijan, arriving at Tashkent at the end of August. They were given a very cool reception by the Bolsheviks, but said that the British Consul from Kashgar would explain all later on his arrival. As soon as Macartney received the approval of the British Government, he started out and succeeded in completing the journey to Tashkent in just twelve days, arriving there ten days after Bailey and Blacker.

[114] Macartney, G. (1920), 47.

[115] *Ibid.*, 48.

[116] Hopkirk (1994), 34.

[117] Blacker, who referred to Macartney as, 'The Chief', published an account of the journey in, *On Secret Patrol in High Asia*, now almost unreadable, being written in the style of a *Boys' Own Paper* imperial yarn.

[118] Bailey, 54.

[119] Sir Percy Sykes, as quoted in Macartney, G. (1920), 57. (Apparently, Sir Percy said this in the discussion which followed Macartney's lecture on Bolshevism delivered to the Central Asian Society in 1920.)

[120] Hopkirk, 96.

[121] Skrine & Nightingale, 260.

[122] Younghusband Collection, FY 122, as quoted in P. French, 156.

[123] Cruikshank, 133 ff.

[124] Skrine & Nightingale, 261.

[125] Geoffrey Chaucer, 'Prologue' to *The Canterbury Tales.*

INDEX

PUBLICATIONS BY JAMES McCARTHY

Scotland: The Land and its Uses, Edinburgh, UK. Chambers Harrap. 1993.

Scotland, Land and People: An Inhabited Solitude. Edinburgh, UK. Luath Press. 1998.

Wild Scotland. Edinburgh, UK. Luath Press. 1998, revised 2006.

Journey into Africa: The Life and Death of Keith Johnston, Scottish Cartographer and Explorer (1844-79). Latheronwheel, Caithness, UK. Whittles Publishing. 2004.

The Road to Tanganyika: The Diaries of Donald Munro and William McEwan. Kachere Series. Zomba, Malawi. 2006.

Selim Aga Aga: A Slave's Odyssey. Edinburgh, UK. Luath Press. 2007.

Monkey Puzzle Man: Archibald Menzies, Plant Hunter. Dunbeath, Caithness, UK. Whittles Publishing and Royal Botanic Garden Edinburgh. 2008.

Patrick Stewart: A Galloway Hero. Wigtown, UK. GC Books. 2011.

That Curious Fellow: Captain Basil Hall, RN. Dunbeath, Caithness, UK. Whittles Publishing. 2011.

John Richardson: Naturalist of the North. Wigtown, UK. GC Books. 2012.

From the Cree to California: The Remarkable Adventures of William Sloan. (Fiction). Newton Stewart, Wigtownshire, UK. J & B Print. 2014.

The Captain's Conspiracy (E-book), 2014.

ABOUT PROVERSE HONG KONG

Proverse Hong Kong is based in Hong Kong with increasingly strong regional and international connections.

Proverse has published novels, novellas, non-fiction (including autobiography, biography, history, memoirs, sport, travel narratives, fictionalized autobiography), single-author poetry collections, children's, teens / young adult and academic books. Other interests include diaries, and academic works in the humanities, social sciences, cultural studies, linguistics and education. Some Proverse books have accompanying audio texts. Some are translated into Chinese.

Proverse welcomes authors who have a story to tell, wisdom, perceptions or information to convey, a person they want to memorialize, a neglect they want to remedy, a record they want to correct, a strong interest that they want to share, skills they want to teach, and who consciously seek to make a contribution to society in an informative, interesting and well-written way. Proverse works with texts by non-native-speaker writers of English as well as by native English-speaking writers.

The name, "Proverse", combines the words "prose" and "verse" and is pronounced accordingly.

THE PROVERSE PRIZE

The Proverse Prize, an annual international competition for an unpublished book-length work of fiction, non-fiction, or poetry, was established in January 2008. It is open to all who are at least eighteen on the date they sign the entry form and without restriction of nationality, residence or citizenship.

Its objectives are: to encourage excellence and / or excellence and usefulness in publishable written work in the English Language, which can, in varying degrees, "delight and instruct". Entries are invited from anywhere in the world.

Summary Terms and Conditions
(for indication only & subject to revision)

The information below is for guidance only. Please refer to the year-specific Proverse Prize Entry Form & Terms & Conditions, which are uploaded, no later than 30 April each year, onto the Proverse Hong Kong website: <www.proversepublishing.com>.

The free Proverse ENewsletter includes ongoing information about the Proverse Prize. To be put on the ENewsletter mailing-list, please email: info@proversepublishing.com with your request.

The Prize
1) Publication by Proverse Hong Kong, with
2) Cash prize of HKD10,000 (HKD7.80 = approx. US$1.00)

Supplementary editing / publication grants may be made to selected other entrants for publication by Proverse Hong Kong.

Depending on the quality of the work in any year, the prize may be shared by at most two entrants or withheld, as recommended by the judges.

In 2015, the entry fee was: HKD220.00 OR GBP32.00.

Writers are eligible, who are at least eighteen on the date they sign The Proverse Prize entry documents. There is no nationality or residence restriction.

Each submitted work must be an unpublished publishable single-author work of non-fiction, fiction, poetry or a play, the original work of the entrant, and submitted in the English language. School textbooks and plays are ineligible.

Translated work: If the work entered is a translation from a language other than English, both the original work and the translation should be previously unpublished. The submitted work will not be judged as a translation but as an original work.

Extent of the Manuscript: within the range of what is usual for the genre of the work submitted. However, it is advisable that novellas be in the range 35,000 to 50,000 words); other fiction (e.g. novels, short-story collections) and non-fiction (e.g. autobiographies, biographies, diaries, letters, memoirs, essay collections, etc.) should be in the range, 80,000 to 110,000 words. Poetry collections should be in the range, 8,000 to 30,000 words. Other word-counts and mixed-genre submissions are not ruled out.

Writers may choose, if they wish, to obtain the services of an Editor in presenting their work, and should acknowledge this help and the nature and extent of this help in the Entry Form.

KEY DATES FOR THE PROVERSE PRIZE IN ANY YEAR
(subject to confirmation and/or change)

Receipt of Entry Fees / Entry Documents	14 April to 31 May of the year of entry
Receipt of entered manuscripts	1 May to 30 June of the year of entry
Announcement of long-list	July-September of the year of entry
Announcement of short-list	October-December of the year of entry
Announcement of winner/ max two winners (sharing the cash prize)	December of the year of entry to April of the year that follows the year of entry (e.g. for entries in May/June 2011, from December 2011 to April 2012)
Cash Award Made	At the same time as publication of the work(s) adjudged the winner / joint-winners of the Proverse Prize
Publication of winning work(s)	In or after November of the year that follows the year of entry (e.g. for entries in May/June 2015, in or after November 2016 onwards)

FIND OUT MORE ABOUT OUR AUTHORS
AND BOOKS

Visit our website
<http://www.proversepublishing.com>

Visit our distributor's website
<www.chineseupress.com>

Follow us on Twitter
Follow news and conversation:
<twitter.com/Proversebooks>
OR
Copy and paste the following to your browser window and
follow the instructions:
https://twitter.com/#!/ProverseBooks

Request our ENewsletter
Send your request to info@proversepublishing.com.

Availability
Most books are available in Hong Kong and world-wide
from our Hong Kong based Distributor,
The Chinese University Press of Hong Kong,
The Chinese University of Hong Kong, Shatin, NT,
Hong Kong SAR, China.
Email: cup-bus@cuhk.edu.hk

All titles are available from Proverse Hong Kong
and the Proverse Hong Kong UK-based Distributor.

We have stock-holding retailers in Hong Kong, Singapore
(Select Books), Canada (Elizabeth Campbell Books),
Principality of Andorra (Llibreria La Puça, La Llibreria).
Orders can be made from bookshops in the UK.

Ebooks
Most of our titles are available also as Ebooks.

CPSIA information can be obtained
at www.ICGtesting.com
Printed in the USA
LVHW02s2038271217
560963LV00011B/1149/P